Design a Right-Minded Team-Building Workshop

12 Steps to Create a Team That Works as One

Third Edition

By
Dan Hogan
Certified Master Facilitator

Books by Dan Hogan

Reason, Ego, & the Right-Minded Teamwork Myth: *The Philosophy and Process for Creating a Right-Minded Team That Works Together as One*

Right-Minded Teamwork in Any Team: *The Ultimate Team Building Method to Create a Team That Works as One*

How to Facilitate Team Work Agreements: *A Practical, 10-Step Process for Building a Right-Minded Team That Works as One*

How to Apply the Right Choice Model: *Create a Right-Minded Team That Works as One*

7 Mindfulness Training Lessons: *Improve Teammates' Ability to Work as One with Right-Minded Thinking*

Right-Minded Teamwork: *9 Right Choices for Building a Team That Works as One*

Design a Right-Minded, Team-Building Workshop: *12 Steps to Create a Team That Works as One*

Achieve Your Organization's Strategic Plan: *Create a Right-Minded Team Management System to Ensure All Teams Work as One*

Acknowledgments & Appreciations

To the thousands of teammates, team leaders,
and team-building facilitators with whom I've
worked with over the last 40 years,

Thank You

for being my teacher.

Collectively, we created this
awesome team-building program.

Right-Minded Teamwork is a business-oriented,
psychological approach to team building where
acceptance, forgiveness, and adjustment
are teammate characteristics,
and customer satisfaction
is the team's result.

In addition, there are several special people I want to joyfully acknowledge and thank for their contributions.

First and foremost, I want to convey my deep and heartfelt gratitude to our editor, Erin Leigh. Thanks to her superb editing and vital guidance, Right-Minded Teamwork is now much easier to understand and successfully integrate in your team. Thank you, Erin. The RMT book series would not have happened without you.
(To contact Erin, email erin@thechoice.life.)

Next, a giant thank you to the Ebook Launch team. Dane Low, our book cover designer, created exceptional cover designs for the Right-Minded Teamwork book series. Thank you for elevating Right-Minded Teamwork. (To reach Dane visit EbookLaunch.com.)

Another sincere thank you goes out to Cathi Bosco, our graphic artist, who renovated and modernized many of our Right-Minded Teamwork process models, graphics, and illustrations
(reach her at CathiBosco.com).
And I also want to thank the Media A-Team, who created the original and current versions of the Right Choice Model
(find them at Mediaateam.com).

Finally, I want to express my gratitude to Jackie D'Elia, our website and UX designer, who successfully modernized the RightMindedTeamwork.com website into an easy-to-use platform. Her work allows us to share the RMT books, models, and other resources and materials with the world. Thank you, Jackie.
(Contact Jackie at JackieDElia.com.)

CONTENTS

How to Design a
Right-Minded
TEAMWORK
Team-Building Workshop:
12-Step Process

Contract:
Designing
the Workshop

1
Start with the
End in Mind
▼
Leader
Defines
Purpose

Leader Meets
Facilitator 2
▼
Shares
Purpose
&
Outcomes

Wants vs. Needs
▼
Facilitator 3
Uncovers
Root Causes

12
Leader &
Facilitator
Begin Designing
the
Second
Workshop

Facilitator Presents
First Draft
Plan to Leader
4

11
Track & Report
Progress for
the Next 90 Days

Leader Announces
Workshop &
Prepares
Teammates

Carry On:
Continuing
After the
Workshop

10
Achieve
Workshop
Outcomes

5
Facilitator
Conducts
Right-Minded
Teamwork
Survey

Commence:
Facilitating
the
Workshop

9
Leader &
Facilitator
Finalize Agenda
&
Workshop
Plan

Facilitator
Presents
Second Draft
Plan
to Leader
8

Facilitator
Interviews
All
Teammates
7

6

Preface

Welcome to Right-Minded Teamwork (RMT).

What is RMT?

Right-Minded Teamwork is an intelligent and empowering teamwork system that creates a *team that works together as one*.

It is everyone's right to work together as *one unified team*, and every person may exercise their right – right now if they choose. That is why RMT is for everyone, everywhere, forever, and it is available to you right now.

Dear Reader, apply RMT and you will improve your work processes and strengthen your relationships.

Apply RMT, and your team will achieve 100% customer satisfaction.

Apply RMT, and your team will *work together as one*.

You'll also do your part to make the world a better place for everyone, everywhere, forever. Let's get started right now.

It is an honor to introduce you to RMT's unique **12 step process in how to design a real-world workshop**. This method has improved the lives and teams of thousands of people worldwide.

Apply this design process in your team-building facilitation, and you, too, will reap its benefits.

Before we get started, let me go over a few things that may be on your mind.

Overview

This book and the online training program - *I'll tell you about the training in a moment* – will teach you how to design practical, powerful workshops using Right-Minded Teamwork's 12 Steps formula.

The 12-step process includes three phases:

1. **Contract**: Designing the workshop (Steps 1-9)

2. **Commence**: Facilitating the workshop (Step 10)

3. **Carry On**: Keeping up the momentum (Steps 11-12)

In the thirty-five years of my team-building career, I facilitated over 500 teams in seven countries. I worked with many of those teams for several years. I used this process every time. Even though they may not have even recognized I was applying these steps; every team leader appreciated the structure and thoroughness of this process.

As a result, we consistently designed workshops that teammates could not wait to attend because they knew they were going to get real work done. And they did!

In our book, **Right-Minded Teamwork in Any Team**: *The Ultimate Team Building Method to Create a Team That Works as One*, I shared the following RMT definition.

> *Right-Minded Teamwork (RMT) is a business-oriented, psychological approach to team building where **acceptance**, **forgiveness**, and **adjustment** are teammate characteristics, and 100% customer satisfaction is the team's result.*

When you apply the 12 steps in designing your workshops, you practically guarantee teammates will strengthen their ability to **accept**, **forgive** and **adjust** to challenging team situations. At the same time, they increase their likelihood of achieving 100% customer satisfaction.

Choose Your Path

You have two options for learning this team-building approach.

1. Book Only
2. Book, Online Course, and Reusable Resources & Templates

Book Only

This is a comprehensive field guide with detailed instructions.

By following the directions in this book on how to apply the 12 Steps, you and your team will design a custom workshop that teammates can't wait to attend because they know they will get real work done.

Book, Online Course, and Reusable Resources & Templates

If you're looking for more than this comprehensive field guide, you may benefit from the enhanced training package.

This upgrade includes:
- Private, unlimited access to an online training class with over two hours of audio instruction
- In the online course, I will expand the concepts presented here
- You will receive a *Reusable Resources & Template* document with checklists and a team survey you can use and reuse

If you purchased this book elsewhere, you could also have the online course and reusable templates for a special discounted price only available at RightMindedTeamwork.com. If you are interested, go to the **Resources** section of this book for all the details.

What makes RMT's 12 step process unique?

I have never seen another real-world team-building process like RMT or its companion 12 step design process in my entire team-building career. (And I've looked, I promise).

If there is another method out there, that is wonderful. Please let me know. But for now, you have, in your hands, a method that will ensure you don't miss any step towards designing a workshop your teammates cannot wait to attend.

What Is in This Book

First, I will explain the **art** and **science** of facilitation and how one succeeds as a team-building facilitator.

After that, I will briefly discuss the range of team-building exercise options available to you, ending in what is your best option - *the real-world approach.*

And yes, Right-Minded Teamwork is a real-world approach. I'll introduce you to the 5 Elements of RMT, the philosophy behind this powerful and continuous improvement method, along with a successful implementation plan.

And for senior team leaders who want to apply RMT across your organization, I will briefly describe RMT's *Team Management System* and how you can learn more.

All of the above helps to establish the context for the rest of the book.

After that, I'll give you an overview of the 12 steps and then immediately discuss each step one at a time.

In the final two sections, you will find a Glossary of Terms & Resources plus a robust collection of templates, checklists, and team exercises. You will also find four successful team implementation stories that would be well worth your study.

· · · · ·

But next, let me share *your new special function* with you.

Welcome to Your New Role: RMT Facilitator

Now that you have a clearer sense of the journey we'll be taking together through these pages, I want to take a moment to congratulate you on your new role. Incorporating RMT's 12-Step design process into your team-building repertoire means **you are now a Right-Minded Teamwork Facilitator.**

As an RMT Facilitator, **your specialty is team transformations**.

Using RMT, you help to transform dysfunctional souls into healthy and functional teammates. You guide teammates to convert their mistakes into Right-Minded attitudes and behaviors. They express their deep and heartfelt gratitude for your facilitation efforts and results. Some even say you "saved them," continuing to seek your support for years to come.

Whether you're new to facilitation or continuing to build your team-building toolkit, add RMT to your practice today. There's no reason not to: All parts of Right-Minded Teamwork, including these 12-Steps, are available for your use. There are no licensing or certification requirements.

My Special Support Function

It took countless workshops, a 35-year career in active team-building facilitation, and the collective wisdom of so many teammates and team leaders to conceptualize and build Right-Minded Teamwork into the robust model it is today.

Though I no longer facilitate actively, choosing to pass that torch on to the next generation of facilitators, I will always continue to promote Right-Minded Teamwork.

The reason for my continued passion is quite simple. I know, beyond a shadow of a doubt, that RMT and these 12-Steps are right for every team, everywhere, forever. If you use them, they *will* help make your client team(s) and world a better place.

To make that happen, though, **your clients need you to show them and their teams the Right-Minded Teamwork way.**

As you lead them down the RMT path, remember: I am here to support you. So, reach out to me. Ask me questions. Let me get to know you so I can refer you to clients looking for an RMT Facilitator.

Also remember that even though you will undoubtedly help your client teams achieve an "early win," creating and sustaining Right-Minded Teamwork takes at least a year.

So, as you enter into the team-building process, stick with it for the long haul. Plan to stay with your team(s) for at least one to two years. Help them firmly establish RMT in their team. Give them the foundation they need to learn, grow, and succeed.

As you do, you will do your part to make the world a better place for everyone, everywhere, forever.

Let's get started now.

Dan Hogan

About Team-Building Facilitation

Team-building facilitation is both **art** and **science**.

The "art" of facilitation is your ability to interact well with teammates - in other words, your ability to lead by example.

When you exhibit Right-Minded Teamwork Attitudes & Behaviors (see a list of 30 below), you teach others emotionally mature teamwork behavior.

You show them exactly how to work and behave as a high-functioning, Right-Minded teammate.

If not…

Displaying egotistical or arrogant behavior inevitably angers teammates and creates teammate resistance. Not leading by example harms the team-building effort.

The best facilitators always keep improving their own interaction and communication skills. They know doing so helps them succeed and serve their teams better.

The "science" of facilitation is your knowledge of the best teamwork methods.

You understand how teams operate. You know how to approach problems strategically. You see the value of guiding teams through a continuous improvement process, like the 5 Elements of Right-Minded Teamwork.

But science isn't just knowledge. It's also a methodology in action.

It is successfully applying Right-Minded Teamwork's 12 Steps to design a real-world, customized, practical team-building workshop.

And it's about facilitating that workshop to produce significant, tangible results.

Succeeding as a Facilitator

Facilitators apply their expertise within three specific functions:
1. Designing Workshops
2. Facilitating Workshops
3. Teaching in Workshops

The most successful facilitators are skilled at the art of communication and the science of facilitation. They readily integrate both into everything they do.

Successful facilitators also do not over-function. "Over-functioning" means doing way too much for teammates (usually things teammates need to do for themselves).

As the story goes, if you give a man a fish, you feed him for a day. If you teach him how to fish, you feed him for a lifetime. Teams need tools, not quick fixes. Be helpful, but don't over-function.

Designing transformational, team-building workshops is an excellent place to start.

From Worst to Best: Team Building Exercises

Team building sounds simple. How can so many people still get it wrong? Here is a list of the team-building exercises options available to you from the worst to the best method.

Worst of the worst...

> In Alison Green's article, *10 Horrifying Teambuilding Exercises*, you can read about some foolish and irrational activities that are called "team building." You can find a link to it at RightMindedTeamwork.com/blog. Look for *"10 Worst Team-Building Exercises."*

> Please discourage others from thinking these activities are worthwhile team-building exercises. They are not.

A little better...

> Some well-meaning people believe happy hours, bowling, or similar activities serve as "team building."

> These are nice social events, and they can certainly encourage camaraderie. But please, don't call them team building. They, too, are not.

Hit or miss...

> In "experiential play" scenarios, teammates typically go to an outdoor playground-type facility. Together, they experience either low-element games (played on the ground) or high-element exercises (constructed on poles).

In these settings, the teacher is accountable for providing a successful experience.

Ideally, participants gain new understandings from their time together that will benefit them and the team in the workplace. In reality, though, while some team members may enjoy the experience, many do not.

Other team activities, such as games, can be fun. But just like the outdoor play activities like the Egg Drop game are not authentic team building, and their results are limited.

Can be helpful...

Educational and training events can be helpful for teams. In this team-building approach, teammates attend a lecture.

For example, an instructor might teach guidelines for resolving work process problems using the Six-Sigma method. Or they might explain one of the personality type style indicators, like DiSC.

Once again, the instructor is responsible for creating a successful training experience.

The hope is that participants will use the guidelines they have learned to build better teamwork. Sometimes this works. Sometimes it doesn't.

Best of the best: Real-World Team-Building

Instead of yet another surface-level group bonding activity, teammates attend a custom-designed, Right-Minded Teamwork team-building workshop.

In this workshop, team members discuss and resolve their real teamwork challenges. All exercises and discussions result in practical Work Agreements.

These Work Agreements outline how teammates will work together to achieve their team's business goals while respecting shared psychological values.

With Right-Minded Teamwork, teammates and the facilitator are jointly held accountable for a successful team-building experience.

Afterward, instead of merely hoping teammates will use their new knowledge on the job, teammates make firm, collective commitments to follow their new Work Agreements to improve their teamwork.

Real progress is made together.

Overview: The 5 Elements of Right-Minded Teamwork

This book specifically covers how to design team-building workshops using RMT's 12 Steps Process.

We'll be diving into Step 1 in just a moment. But before we get there, let me share a little background on Right-Minded Teamwork itself.

The Right-Minded Teamwork model was built and fine-tuned over 35 years of facilitation, development, and team transformation.

The concepts of RMT can be distilled down into the 5 Elements of Right-Minded Teamwork, which consist of two team goals and three team-building methods.

Together, the 5 Elements form a six to 12-month continuous improvement plan with the power to create Right-Minded Teamwork in any team of any size.

Right now, your team may be struggling with issues that feel insurmountable. But with Right-Minded Teamwork, navigating those rough, choppy waters is absolutely possible.

(Hint: Team building workshops, just like the kind you'll soon create using the 12 Steps Process, are an excellent way to introduce the 5 Elements to your team.)

The framework's 5 Elements include two goals and three methods:

1. Team **Business Goal**: Achieve 100% Customer Satisfaction

2. Team **Psychological Goal**: Commit to Right-Minded Thinking

3. Team **Work Agreements**: Create & Follow Commitments

4. **Team Operating System**: Make It Effective & Efficient

5. **Right-Minded Teammates**: Strengthen Individual Performance

Without clear goals, team members may falter, become distracted, or fail to fulfill their role on the team. Goals provide direction and a way to measure progress and success. For this reason, the first two of Right-Minded Teamwork's 5 Elements focus on goal setting.

RMT teaches there are two types of goals every team should consider: **business goals** and **psychological goals**.

In order for a team to succeed, each team member must first know, understand, and choose to align with the team's overarching performance goals (business goals). All team members must also know, understand, and choose to align with the team's interpersonal, behavioral, and communication goals (psychological goals).

By clarifying and communicating the team's business and psychological goals, all team members are offered a level playing field.

Once the team's goals are clear, the next three Elements provide three specific tools to help create a high-performing team.

The three tools in RMT's 5 Element model are:
- Work Agreements
- Team Operating Systems
- Right-Minded Teammates

How do these three tools work?

Firstly, **Work Agreements** are written agreements created collectively by all team members. They define a single set of performance and behavioral expectations. Work Agreements are powerfully effective at resolving interpersonal issues and conflicts because they provide a mutually agreeable baseline for everyone involved.

Once the playing field has been leveled with Work Agreements, a **Team Operating System** defines or redefines the team's structure. A Team Operating System outlines roles, responsibilities, and team processes and procedures.

Lastly, **Right-Minded Teammates** offers teams a way forward by focusing on individual success within the whole. Teammates are encouraged to support one another to reach new heights.

Knowing where the team is headed, how they will be treated, and precisely what is expected of them allows each team member to confidently engage in their role and support the team.

In this way, the 5 Elements provide a firm foundation for team growth.

The 5 Elements model can also serve as a team assessment tool to prepare for and execute a practical team-building workshop to improve team performance. Thinking about each of the Elements within your team and applying the Team Operating System's *Team Performance Factor Assessment* are excellent ways to identify specific team challenges.

The Philosophy Behind the 5 Elements

The philosophy behind RMT's 5 Elements is explained in the short story ***Reason, Ego & the Right-Minded Teamwork Myth***.

This story illustrates where teamwork originally began and how it evolved to where it is today.

As you read, you will realize achieving the Right-Minded Teamwork Myth's ideals is not possible in this world.

However, it is possible to adopt and live ***Right-Minded Attitudes & Behaviors***. Doing so should be your team's psychological goal.

In a few pages, you will find 30 Right-Minded Attitudes & Behaviors you and your teammates can adapt and adopt.

I encourage you to read this story in our book ***Reason, Ego & the Right-Minded Teamwork Myth****: The Philosophy and Process for Creating a Right-Minded Team That Works Together as One*. Pick up your free ebook copy at RightMindedTeamwork.com. It is also available in paperback at your favorite book retailer.

Commit to Your Team's Version of
Right-Minded Thinking

Psychological goals illustrate how your team's behavior and Work Agreements align with your organization's stated values.

To achieve Right-Minded Teamwork, your team must first identify the "right" attitudes for the team. These chosen attitudes form your team's collective, consciously chosen thought system. They describe how you will **do no harm** as you **work as one**.

Your team's initial set of Right-Minded Teamwork attitudes are created and agreed upon during the first RMT team-building workshop. After that, they may be adjusted and updated on an as-needed basis.

Choose Right-Minded Attitudes for Your Team

Your list of "right" attitudes can be short. Here is an example.

We choose these Right-Minded attitudes as our psychological goals:
- *We accept 100% accountability and responsibility for our thoughts and behaviors.*
- *When we make mistakes, we never punish. We learn. We recover. We do no harm. We work as one.*
- *We positively acknowledge and reward each other.*
- *We are we-centered, never self-centered.*
- *When difficult team situations happen, we accept, forgive, and adjust our attitudes and behavior. We always find solutions because we believe that none of us is as smart as all of us.*
- *When new teammates join our team, we will share these goals and ask them to choose them too.*

After you create these values and norms for your team, you must commit to living them. Both the attitudes and the team's commitment to living them are captured in your team's Work Agreements.

Two Options for
Choosing Attitudes & Behaviors

To identify the "right" attitudes and psychological goals for your team, you have two options:

1. Share the **Right-Minded Teammate Attitudes & Behaviors** list with the team; see below and allow teammates to choose a few from that list. Or use those ideas to create goals that fit your team better.

2. Share the **Right Choice Model** (as described in the book *How to Apply the Right Choice Model*. In a team event, agree on a list of accountable attitudes and work behaviors your team believes are needed to address your teamwork issues and sustain RMT successfully.

To Learn More...

To learn more about presenting and teaching the Right Choice Model, go to RightMindedTeamwork.com or your favorite book retailer and pick up your copy of *How to Apply the Right Choice Model: Create a Right-Minded Team That Works as One.* Search for the section, *"How to Present & Apply the Right Choice Model in Your Team."* There, you will be given specific instructions on successfully presenting the Right Choice Model, including how to relate it to your team's current challenge.

30 Right-Minded Teamwork Attitudes & Behaviors

Over decades of team-building work, I worked with hundreds of teams. Along the way, I collected their Right-Minded attitudes and behaviors into a list of choices that I grouped into **work behaviors** and **work processes**. Use this list to either adopt or adapt as your team's Psychological Goals and Work Agreements.

Was I Born with These Thoughts & Attitudes?

Thoughts and attitudes always precede teamwork behavior.

Right-Minded attitudes come from Reason. Wrong-minded attitudes come from Ego.

The good news is that Right-Minded attitudes are natural. They are already inside you and your teammates.

When you think about any of the wrong-minded Ego attitudes listed below, ask yourself,

> *Was I born with these depressing, debilitating, and awful attitudes?*

Your answer will always be **"no!"** You learned those wrong-minded attitudes from Ego. That means *you can unlearn them, too.*

You *Can* Change Your Mind

In 35 years of team-building facilitation, I heard too many well-intentioned albeit wrong-minded teammates say,

> *That's just the way I am. I can't change.*

That is ***simply not true***.

What is true is that they refused to change their minds.

> *When someone says they cannot change, what they are really saying is their behavior is more powerful than their mind.*

When they realize and joyfully accept that ***their mind is in charge***, they have opened the way for happiness, inner peace, and Right-Minded Teamwork.

Why You Want to Change Your Perspective

Fixed perspectives prevent you from achieving Right-Minded Teamwork. Your limiting beliefs, interpretations, and lessons from Ego are blocks to Right-Minded Thinking.

To remove those blocks, you must transform your self-limiting thoughts. The first of RMT's 7 Mindfulness Training Lessons will help you do that.

Lesson one of the 7 Mindfulness Training Lessons states, *"I am never upset for the reason I think."*

Reminding yourself of this truth when you or your teammates are out of your Right Minds will help you experience a **moment of Reason**. Instead of seeing your teammate's behavior as a negative Ego attack, you are able to reinterpret their behavior as a desperate **call for help** from you and your teammates.

With this new insight, you are able to respond to your teammate with Reason's wise guidance. With Reason's help, you have effectively changed your perspective.

· · · · ·

The 30 Right-Minded Teamwork Attitudes & Behaviors starting on the next page will help you change your perspective and achieve Right-Minded Thinking.

Work Behavior Attitudes

As the Decision-Maker, You Behave One Way or the Other!

EGO   DECISION MAKER   REASON

Demonstrate adversarial competition and power struggles	Demonstrate collaborative competition and synergy
Demonstrate victim or victimizer attitudes & behaviors	Exhibit accountable and responsible attitudes & behavior
Worry that "I am my mistakes;" continue to obsess over mistakes	Embrace that "I am not my mistakes;" mistakes are opportunities for me to learn
Noticeable lack of emotional maturity and empathy	Desire to be emotionally mature and compassionate
Exhibit self-centered attitudes	Exhibit we-centered attitudes
Hold & project grievances; Never forget or forgive	Embrace & extend forgiveness; Let go of issues from the past
After mistakes, helplessness occurs, and I choose to give up or not try as hard	After mistakes, forgiveness occurs, and I choose to try again and again

Work Behavior Attitudes (Continued)

There's a mindset of scarcity, a belief that to give is to lose	There's an attitude of abundance, a belief that to give is to receive
There is suspicion, closed-mindedness, and resistance to change	There is readiness and open-mindedness for positive change
Too often, people restate their position, believing they are right, and others are wrong	We always seek mutual understanding: believing together, we are right
I believe I'm the smartest, and I can prove it	We believe none of us is as smart as all of us
I demonstrate a conscious or unconscious attitude of confusion, chaos, complexity, and drama	We continually demonstrate a conscious attitude of clarity, order, simplicity, and calmness
There's a widespread belief that difficult team situations and changes determine how we feel	We know for sure that our minds determine how we feel about difficult situations or changes
We believe it is best to keep quiet when correction is needed	We have a team culture of appropriately speaking up when a correction is needed
We believe in these attitudes: vulnerability, unkindness, hate, attack, blame	We embrace these attitudes: invulnerability, love, kindness, do no harm, work as one

Work Behavior Attitudes (Continued)

We believe in power over others	We believe in power with others
Growth is painful; remember, if there is no pain, there is no gain	Growth doesn't have to be painful; learning is joyously attained and gladly remembered
It is best to do unto others (reject, attack, defend) before they do unto you	We do unto others (accept, forgive, adjust) as we would have them do unto us
There is a feeling of avoidance and criticism among teammates	There is a spirit of acknowledgment and reward among teammates
There is a love and a need for power, fame, money, and pleasure	We strive for non-attachment to power, fame, money, and pleasure
Our team is a battleground where conflict is prolonged as we act like victims or victimizers	Our team is our learning classroom where conflict is resolved as we act like Right-Minded Teammates
There is mistrust, fear, and lack of safety among teammates	There is trust, peace, and safety among teammates
Defensiveness is prevalent in our team	Defenselessness is widespread in our team

Process Behavior Attitudes

Your Team Can Operate One Way or the Other!

The team's purpose, vision, and mission are unclear and not supported	Our team continuously clarifies our purpose, vision, and mission and actively support them
There is no discernable team operating system	There is an efficient, continuous improvement team operating system in place
There is a predominant attitude of avoidance and complaining	We have an attitude and a system for acknowledgment and reward
Disagreements and a lack of clear roles and responsibilities exist	We periodically clarify teammate roles and responsibilities
We are unclear who makes decisions and how	Our team has a clear and effective decision-making Work Agreement
We spend too much time and energy applying inefficient work processes	Our work processes and procedures are clear, understood, accepted, and efficient
Too often, people are punished for making mistakes	We always embrace an attitude of converting mistakes into learning opportunities

The 10 Characteristics of Right-Minded Teammates

In addition to the 30 Right-Minded Attitudes & Behaviors, Right-Minded Teammates live these ten characteristics.

Right-Minded Teammates have many different surface traits and personalities. They are not all alike. They have numerous backgrounds, vastly different experiences, and a wide range of skills.

Nevertheless, it is understood that the Right-Minded Teammate, in their own particular behavioral style, happily live these characteristics because they align the teammate's authentic *self* with their team's version of the RMT motto: *do no harm, work as one*, and *none of us is as smart as all of us*.

1. Trust	2. Honesty	3. Tolerance
4. Gentleness	5. Joy	6. Defenselessness
7. Generosity	8. Patience	9. Open-Mindedness
	10. Faithfulness	

You will find a complete description of these characteristics in RMT's book: ***Right-Minded Teamwork in Any Team:*** *The Ultimate Team Building Method to Create a Team That Works as One.*

Actionable Attitudes = Better Behaviors

These Right-Minded attitudes are practical. However, these noble thoughts and attitudes will do no good unless you discuss them and define what they mean for your team.

Once you have identified and defined the behaviors associated with your chosen attitudes, captured in your team Work Agreements, you must also make the conscious choice to live them going forward.

Don't let your team's insignificant, Ego-driven squabbles pull you down.

Be vigilant and demonstrate by your actions and behaviors that you have risen above your old, petty, teamwork battleground issues.

No team situation can pull you into Ego's realm of conflict when you believe it is far better to collaborate and win than argue and lose.

Remember, it is from your collective Right Mind that you create your Work Agreements. And when you make and follow your promises, you are uniting with each other without the Ego. When you do that, you have returned to the United Circle of Right-Minded Thinking. From that unified circle, it will be much easier to recover from any difficult team situation because you have, at that moment, restored your team's collective Right Mind to Reason.

The Work Agreement Process

Now that teammates have chosen their Right Attitudes & Behaviors, they are prepared to create your Work Agreements.

Nearly all teamwork issues can be addressed and resolved with Work Agreements.

Two Types of Work Agreements

A **process Work Agreement** describes who will do what and the work methods they will use. It defines work tasks in terms of roles, responsibilities, interfaces, or procedures.

One essential process Agreement is a team's Decision-Making Work Agreement. RMT advocates every team create such an Agreement as early as possible. Without one, the team will likely encounter many unnecessary interpersonal dysfunctions and work mistakes. We'll talk more about Decision-Making Agreements in a moment.

A **behavioral Work Agreement** describes how people will behave while they perform their tasks, such as the ways teammates will bring to light, communicate, and resolve difficult performance issues or interpersonal conflicts. This type of Work Agreement aims for transparency in all such interactions.

A Work Agreement that is wholeheartedly agreed upon includes an **Intention** statement that defines your team's choice as well as **Clarifications or Conditions** for acceptance. Here is an example.

. . . . .

Intention:
1. Each teammate will communicate their thoughts and feelings in appropriate ways.

Clarifications or Conditions:
A. We follow the spirit and intent of our company values.
B. If we believe another person is communicating inappropriately, we will call it to their attention in private.
C. Even though this Agreement addresses inappropriate communication behaviors, we also agree to give positive teammate reinforcement when we see and hear excellent communication.

Below you will find two real examples of Work Agreements. The first one is a **behavioral** team communication Work Agreement. The other is a **process** Work Agreement around decision-making.

I worked with this team for a few years. These were phenomenally successful Work Agreements because teammates passionately created and actively lived them day in and day out.

The communication Work Agreement directly below is also used as a teaching device in this book. In the pages to come, I will show you how that team created this Agreement.

Real Team Work Agreements

Behavioral Agreement – Communication

Team Choice: Intention Statement

1. Each teammate will communicate in a respectful way.

Clarifications / Conditions for Acceptance:

A. We will use good communication techniques that include appropriate body language and tone of voice, plus suitable words.
B. If we see or hear disrespect or we hear an inappropriate behind-the-back conversation, we own it and need to step in.
C. If someone unintentionally shows disrespect, we will give them the benefit of the doubt, let them know, and create a new way to interact going forward.
D. We will actively support team decisions in word, deed, and energy; we will use our decision-making protocol agreement for key decisions.
E. We will be on time for meetings.
F. We will ask, "May I interrupt you?"
G. We will use observable facts during disagreements and decision-making, and we will acknowledge when we are using assumptions.
H. We will understand each other's roles, ask for help if we need it, share relevant information and if helpful, give constructive feedback in private.
I. If someone continues to break this agreement, we will tell them that we will invite a third party to help if there is continued disagreement. If that doesn't solve the issues, we will all go to a higher authority for support and resolution.

Decision-Making Work Agreements

A team's Decision-Making Work Agreement clearly defines how decisions are made and who makes them. If your team does not already have a Decision-Making Work Agreement, decision-making is an excellent topic to choose as the teamwork topic to address in your first Work Agreements workshop.

RMT advocates every team create such a Decision-Making Work Agreement as early as possible. Without one, the team will likely encounter many unnecessary interpersonal dysfunctions and work mistakes. I'm confident your own experience has already shown you this is true, which is why it makes good business sense to create one and include it in your team's Operating System.

It's also a good idea in team meetings to remind teammates of your Decision-Making Work Agreement. Doing so will prevent many conflicts.

If you do not currently have a Decision-Making Agreement or you have not updated yours lately, make it a priority.

Below you will find a description of several different decision-making approaches. Use these options to help you create an effective Agreement for your team.

Range of Decision-Making Options

There is no one right way to construct your Decision-Making Agreement, but here are some guidelines and definitions that will help.

1. Command

In this option, the leader decides and announces their decision to teammates. This option is suitable for emergency situations and inconsequential types of decisions. Ideally, when the leader announces their choice, teammates will happily abide by the leader's decision.

2. Consult

The leader gathers information and recommendations in small group meetings or with others outside the team. As with the command option, teammates happily abide by the decision when the leader announces their choice.

3. Consensus

In this option, the team desires to reach a consensus. Everyone has equal authority to persuade and advocate for what they believe to be the best decision.

Consensus does not mean that everyone agrees. What it means is that everyone will *actively support* the decision in word and deed even if they did not get everything they wanted. By actively supporting the decision, teammates are *living* their RMT motto of *"none of us is as smart as all of us."*

Before the team discusses an issue, create a fallback decision-making option if the team cannot reach a consensus. For example, you might agree that the majority of votes wins. Or you could default to a Subject Matter Expert or the team leader to make the final decision in the case of no consensus. There is no perfect fallback, but having one before discussing the problem that needs a decision is highly recommended.

4. Delegation

In this option, the leader gives the team or a subgroup the authority to decide *if* they adhere to specific guidelines and boundaries.

When the group announces their choice, the leader and teammates will abide by the group's decision.

Decision-Making Guidelines

Use some or all of these guidelines in your team Decision-Making Work Agreement.

An effective Decision-Making Work Agreement requires facilitating the team through two different activities. First, *define the problem* and, second, *solve the problem.*

For important decisions, always allow enough time to discuss the issue thoroughly to ensure you properly define the problem.

Frequently remind teammates of your RMT motto: **None of us is as smart as all of us**.

It's best to avoid debates. If you decide to play a devil's advocate role, announce it in advance.

It's also best not to immediately settle for majority rule, compromises, or trade-offs. Always go into every discussion by looking for a win-win solution.

It's best not to interpret a teammate's silence as support. For some decisions, ask each person to state out loud why they support the decision.

Decide what the group will tell others outside the team about the decision. If necessary, script a standard communication that all agree to follow.

Once they make the decision, the team must reach a consensus.

What Is Consensus?

Consensus is not the same as 100% agreement. It does mean that all teammates agree to *actively support the team's decision,* in word and deed, even though it might not be their personal choice.

How do you know you have reached a consensus? Each teammate can say with confidence:

> *My personal views and ideas have been listened to and seriously considered.*
>
> *I have openly listened to and seriously considered the ideas and views of every other team member.*
>
> *Whether or not this decision would have been my choice, I will actively support it and work towards its implementation and success.*

An Actual Decision-Making Work Agreement

In this book, you will find two real-world Work Agreement examples.

The first one is a behavioral Communication Agreement, and the other is the **Decision-Making Work Agreement** below.

I worked with this team for a few years. They were phenomenally successful because teammates passionately created and actively lived their Agreements day in and day out.

Process Agreement – Decision-Making Protocol

Team Choice: Intention Statement

2. We will go for consensus for all key team decisions, but our fallback will be that Maria [team leader] will decide if we cannot reach a consensus.

Conditions for Acceptance / Clarification

A. Before entering a discussion, we'll agree on the decision-making method and fall back, plus when [date] a decision will be made.

B. Before delving into a solution, we will create an opportunity or problem statement.

C. At the beginning of our discussion, we will determine boundaries & givens (i.e., time sensitivity; cost, hassle, impact, 80% or 100% perfect decision, etc.).

D. We provide a business case (appropriate justification) for our decision, including cost/benefit.

E. During our conversations, we will advocate and inquire. We will not hold back. For instance, we will acknowledge assumptions and facts.

F. To create the best solutions, we will also think about alternative ways to test our solution (Devil's Advocate).

G. If we find ourselves at an impasse, we will call a "time out" to calm down or acquire more technical information.

H. When a decision is made, we will accurately represent and support the decision.

I. We do this agreement because we want to improve teamwork and trust in one another.

J. We will hold ourselves and others accountable for living the letter and the spirit of this agreement; we will fine-tune it as necessary

5 Elements:
RMT Implementation Plan

Three Workshops + 90-Day Operating System

Overview

There is no one right way to implement RMT in your *Team Management System*; however, the three-workshop plan presented here has proven effective countless times in single teams.

These sequential actions will ensure you succeed in creating a *team that works together as one.*

Workshop Preparation & Team Orientation Meeting
- Team Leader & Facilitator prepare for team orientation
- Conduct a short Team Orientation meeting and assign teammate preparation tasks

First Workshop – Work Agreements
- Identify team psychological goals and values (Element #2)
- Create at least one team Work Agreement (Element #3)
- Identify 2 or 3 improvement projects for the next 90 days

Second Workshop – Operating System
- Reset and reaffirm business goals (Element #1) and agree on the Team Operating System (Element #4)

Third Workshop - Teammates
- Conduct a Right-Minded Teammate development workshop (Element #5).

90-Day Operating Plan - Ongoing
- Every 90 days, conduct another *Team Performance Factor Assessment,* and then the team meets to assess progress, identify opportunities, take action, and achieve new teamwork improvements.

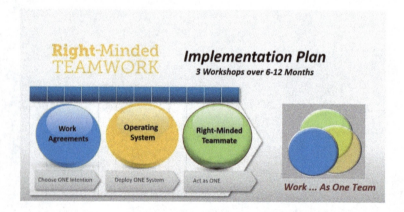

Workshop Preparation & Team Orientation Meeting

The team leader and the team-building facilitator will prepare for their team's RMT Team Orientation meeting and then conduct the meeting

They will determine to conduct an in-person event or a virtual workshop. If they hold a virtual workshop, the same principles, concepts, and steps apply.

However, **an in-person workshop is highly recommended**. Being physically in the same room gives teammates a chance to see and feel other teammates' attitudes and behaviors.

If a virtual format is necessary, use a video software conferencing platform to ensure all participants can see each other and the virtual flip chart you will use to capture your team Work Agreements.

It's essential as one of your first steps to assess your team's current performance. This could be a subjective or an objective assessment. The facilitator will offer using the RMT *Team Performance Factor Assessment* that is discuss in Element #4 – Team Operating System.

In the orientation meeting, teammates will discuss and understand the RMT 5 Element process, the three-workshop implementation, the 90-day ongoing process, and the creation of team Work Agreements that will help them improve their teamwork.

Teammates learn the facilitator will guide the team in the first three workshops and co-facilitate their fourth. At that time, the facilitator will turn over the facilitation duties to the team going forward.

The leader and facilitator will facilitate a team discussion about choosing the teammate's two or three teamwork topics to address in their first workshop. Teammates learn the facilitator will interview them before the first workshop, and collectively, they will finalize the first topics to address. They also agree on the first workshop date.

Teammates are asked to read ***Right-Minded Teamwork***: *9 Right Choices for Building a Team That Works as One*. Doing so is optional, but this short and easy-to-read book will help foster an attitude of "Right-Mindedness" among all teammates.

Workshop 1 – Psychological Goals & Work Agreements

Under your leader or a facilitator's guidance, your team works together to clarify and agree on its psychological goals or team values and create one or more Work Agreements to address the two teamwork topics chosen in the orientation meeting.

Work Agreements, created collectively by and agreed upon by all team members, ensure everyone operates under a single set of performance and behavioral expectations. They are powerfully effective at resolving interpersonal issues and work process conflicts.

When your team creates and follows its first set of Agreements, it is an "early win" for the team because teammates resolve essential issues while also setting a positive, we-can-do-this tone for future successes.

Here's a real "early win" story. Look for **Example #3 – International Project Team,** in the RMT Implementation Plan – 4 Actual Examples section at the end of this book. This major capital project team immediately saved $10,000 a week in labor costs when they successfully used RMT's **process Work Agreement** to streamline their meetings. Furthermore, all four examples will show you clear evidence that Work Agreements work.

But to help you on your way to achieving an "early win," you can **use the list of 30 Right-Minded Teamwork Attitudes & Behaviors**, discussed later, to help you choose your team's goals and desired work behaviors.

The first workshop typically focuses on team cohesion and unity. Often a lack of cohesion or unity is the underlying cause of poor performance that created your team's improvement opportunities.

Teams often experience a boost in productivity and motivation from the first workshop alone because they immediately see the positive benefits of the Right-Minded Teamwork model.

Workshop 2 – Business Goals & Operating System

Once psychological goals and initial Work Agreements are in place, you are ready for the second workshop. This event, which takes place four to eight weeks after the first workshop, revolves around clarifying your business goal and establishing an effective Team Operating System.

Often, the business goal is to achieve 100% customer satisfaction. If so, your team must agree on what this kind of success looks like for your customer. Additionally, it is crucial that you validate your conclusions with your team's customers.

Validating your assumptions means ensuring all teammates know and understand not only the expectations of your team's direct customers but also the expectations of *their customers*.

*When your team helps your customers achieve 100% satisfaction with **their customers**, you will most certainly have achieved a prosperous and successful working relationship.*

You will find instructions for **Creating a Customer Satisfaction Plan** in *Right-Minded Teamwork in Any Team: The Ultimate Team-Building Method to Create a Team That Works as One.*

With a clear business goal and united focus, you are ready to discuss and create an actionable plan to strengthen work performance and eliminate wasted time and effort.

In this second team-building workshop, you will identify one to three opportunities to improve your **Team Operating System** over the next 90 days.

Just as Work Agreements guide team behavior, the Team Operating System defines (or redefines) your team's structure. The system includes a *Team Performance Factor Assessment* that helps your team identify improvement opportunities such as roles, responsibilities, and team processes and procedures. In Element #4, you will learn more about RMT's 90-Day Team Operating System and how to use it.

This second workshop continues to build momentum by delivering more evidence that the RMT model is working.

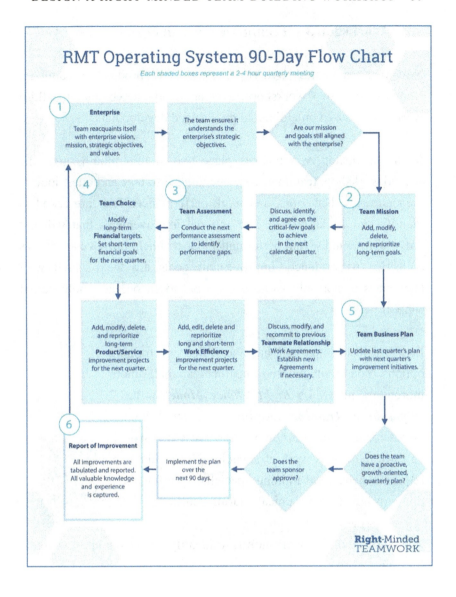

RMT Operating System 90-Day Flow Chart

Each shaded boxes represent a 2-4 hour quarterly meeting

1 Enterprise
Team reacquaints itself with enterprise vision, mission, strategic objectives, and values.

The team ensures it understands the enterprise's strategic objectives.

Are our mission and goals still aligned with the enterprise?

4 Team Choice
Modify long-term **Financial** targets. Set short-term financial goals for the next quarter.

3 Team Assessment
Conduct the next performance assessment to identify performance gaps.

Discuss, identify, and agree on the critical-few goals to achieve in the next calendar quarter.

2 Team Mission
Add, modify, delete, and reprioritize long-term goals.

Add, modify, delete, and reprioritize long-term **Product/Service** improvement projects for the next quarter.

Add, edit, delete and reprioritize long and short-term **Work Efficiency** improvement projects for the next quarter.

Discuss, modify, and recommit to previous **Teammate Relationship** Work Agreements. Establish new Agreements if necessary.

5 Team Business Plan
Update last quarter's plan with next quarter's improvement initiatives.

6 Report of Improvement
All improvements are tabulated and reported. All valuable knowledge and experience is captured.

Implement the plan over the next 90 days.

Does the team sponsor approve?

Does the team have a proactive, growth-oriented, quarterly plan?

Right-Minded
TEAMWORK

Workshop 3 – Teammate Growth & Development

Now that teammates have experienced more productive teamwork from the first two workshops, you are ready to conduct the third workshop focused on individual growth and development.

In this workshop, which takes place two to four months after the second workshop, teammates are encouraged to take an honest look at their attitudes, behaviors, and work performance. They are asked to identify simple, legitimate, and actional improvements that will not only improve individual performance but will help improve the team's collective performance. Improvement goals are then shared with teammates to not only validate them but to encourage wholehearted support.

For this workshop, you have a variety of training options. You might choose to instruct teammates more thoroughly in RMT's **Right Choice Model** or the *7 Mindfulness Training Lessons*. You could invite a professional to teach a new work process that would enhance the team's work efficiencies. You could also request a behavioral training specialist to teach such things as how to communicate during conflicts.

The outcome of this workshop is to identify actionable improvements for each person.

After you complete your third RMT workshop, you and your teammates will be totally convinced that your Team Operating System, Work Agreements, and customer satisfaction mission will ensure you create and sustain Right-Minded Teamwork.

Approximately 90 days after your third workshop (and every 90 days after that), your team will follow your Team Operating Plan (created in the second workshop) to assess team progress, identify new improvement opportunities, take action, and achieve greater team success.

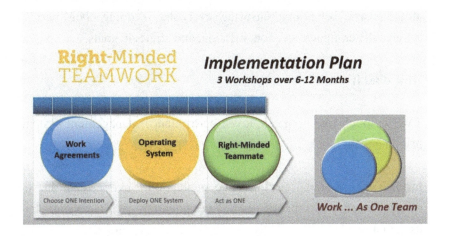

90-Day Operating Plan - Ongoing

- Every 90 days, conduct another *Team Performance Factor Assessment,* and then the team meets to assess progress, identify opportunities, take action, and achieve new teamwork improvements.

 To Learn More...

For four real-world success stories illustrating this multi-workshop plan, go to the Resources section at the end of this book and find **RMT Implementation Plan – 4 Actual Examples**.

Achieve Your Organization's Strategic Plan with Right-Minded Teamwork

What is the Enterprise-Wide **Team Management System** (TMS)?

An enterprise's Team Management System (TMS) aligns all teammate attitudes and behaviors, ensuring everyone is doing their part to achieve the company's vision, mission, and strategic goals.

How does it work?

TMS is much like your employee performance management system, just on a team level.

Instead of individual performance evaluations, every team in the enterprise sets performance goals. Every quarter, each team measures its actual results.

What are the benefits?

Every team in the enterprise operates with clarity and focus. The enterprise consistently achieves a higher percentage of its strategic goals year over year.

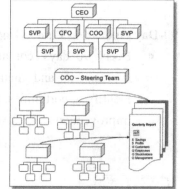

How long does it take to see the benefits?

Within the first six to twelve months, TMS will begin paying for itself. Within eighteen to twenty-four months, TMS will report consistent and demonstrable enterprise-wide results.

Who participates?

Executive Leadership
TMS Steering Team
Internal team building facilitators
All teams will eventually participate

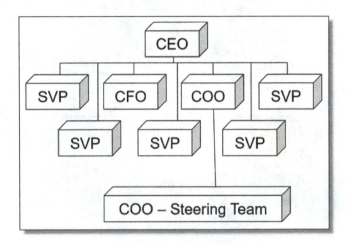

 To Learn More…

To learn more about this system, go to RightMindedTeamwork.com or your favorite book retailer and pick up your copy of ***Achieve Your Organization's Strategic Plan:*** *Create a Right-Minded Team Management System to Ensure All Teams Work as One.*

How to Design a
Right-Minded
TEAMWORK
Team-Building Workshop:
12-Step Process

Contract: Designing the Workshop

1 Start with the End in Mind ▼ Leader Defines Purpose

2 Leader Meets Facilitator ▼ Shares Purpose & Outcomes

3 Wants vs. Needs ▼ Facilitator Uncovers Root Causes

4 Facilitator Presents First Draft Plan to Leader

5 Leader Announces Workshop & Prepares Teammates

6 Facilitator Conducts Right-Minded Teamwork Survey

7 Facilitator Interviews All Teammates

8 Facilitator Presents Second Draft Plan to Leader

9 Leader & Facilitator Finalize Agenda & Workshop Plan

Commence: Facilitating the Workshop

10 Achieve Workshop Outcomes

Carry On: Continuing After the Workshop

11 Track & Report Progress for the Next 90 Days

12 Leader & Facilitator Begin Designing the Second Workshop

Introducing the
12 Step Design Process

Your client wants help. You know their needs. How can you ensure you deliver a truly transformational workshop experience?

This book will teach you how to design practical, powerful team-building workshops using Right-Minded Teamwork's proven 12 Steps formula.

The 12 Steps Workshop Design Process includes three phases:

Contract: Designing the workshop (steps 1-9)

Commence: Facilitating the workshop (step 10)

Carry On: Keeping up momentum after the workshop (steps 11-12)

Contract: Designing the Workshop

. . . . . .

Step 1:

The team leader determines the workshop's purpose. Often workshops focus on something the team needs to change or improve because teammates are not working well together.

Step 2:

The team leader connects with the team building facilitator to convey the workshop's purpose and potential outcomes. Both agree to follow Right-Minded Teamwork's 12 Steps Process.

Step 3:

The leader gives the facilitator permission to think of their initial desired outcomes as symptoms, allowing the facilitator to uncover root causes the leader may not have considered. It's not unusual between steps 3 & 7 to learn that what the leader said they initially wanted may not be what the team needs.

Step 4:

The facilitator creates and presents a 1st Draft Plan to the leader. The plan includes the initial set of workshop outcomes, agenda, Punch List of workshop topics, and an announcement plan.

Step 5:

The leader announces the workshop and prepares teammates. Teammates learn the facilitator will interview them. By offering their input and perspective, they will participate in designing the workshop outcomes and agenda.

Step 6:

The facilitator conducts a Right-Minded teammate survey to help identify potential workshop outcomes.

Step 7:

The facilitator interviews all teammates, summarizing their collective views in the Punch List document.

Step 8:

The facilitator creates and presents a 2nd Draft Plan to the leader.

Step 9:

The leader and facilitator fine-tune and agree on the final outcomes and workshop agenda. Together, they distribute the agenda and begin preparing teammates for the workshop.

Commence: Facilitating the Workshop

Step 10:

The leader and facilitator conduct the workshop and achieve workshop outcomes.

Teammates agree to track their performance after the workshop. They agree on what they will track, how they will track it, and to whom they will report their progress. They agree to conduct team-building workshops every 90-days.

Carry On: Keeping Up Momentum

Step 11:

For the next 90 days, the team tracks their progress.

Step 12:

The leader and facilitator either begin designing the second workshop or transfer that responsibility to others.

If the facilitator is asked to design the next workshop, the cycle continues onward, beginning with Step 1 again.

As the cycle is repeated over time, the team grows and evolves together.

Step-by-Step Detailed Instruction

Watch Training Videos, Too

If you purchased the book package from RightMindedTeamwork.com, you were enrolled automatically in an online training class with 2 hours of audio instruction where I share practical concepts and tips on how to apply every step.

But if you purchased this book elsewhere, you could also have the training class and reusable material for a special discounted price at RightMindedTeamwork.com.

Go to RightMindedTeamwork.com and search for the *Reusable Resources & Templates* for *Design a Right-Minded, Team-Building Workshop* to obtain these valuable resources.

Watch the videos to enhance your learning experience of each step.

How to Design a
Right-Minded
TEAMWORK
Team-Building Workshop:
12-Step Process

Contract:
Designing
the Workshop

1 Start with the
End in Mind
▼
Leader
Defines
Purpose

2 Leader Meets
Facilitator
▼
Shares
Purpose
&
Outcomes

3 Wants vs. Needs
▼
Facilitator
Uncovers
Root Causes

4 Facilitator Presents
First Draft
Plan to Leader

5 Leader Announces
Workshop &
Prepares
Teammates

6 Facilitator
Conducts
Right-Minded
Teamwork
Survey

7 Facilitator
Interviews
All
Teammates

8 Facilitator
Presents
Second Draft
Plan
to Leader

9 Leader &
Facilitator
Finalize Agenda
&
Workshop
Plan

10 Achieve
Workshop
Outcomes

11 Track & Report
Progress for
the Next 90 Days

12 Leader &
Facilitator
Begin Designing
the
Second
Workshop

Carry On:
Continuing
After the
Workshop

Commence:
Facilitating
the
Workshop

Step 1 – Start with the End in Mind

This step begins when the team leader contacts you, asking you to design and facilitate a team-building workshop.

The leader shares their workshop goals. You accept the assignment.

You both agree to meet and discuss the team-building plan.

All you know, at this point, is that the team needs to improve something or address a specific challenge, such as:

- merging or reorganizing two previously independent teams into one unified group, or

- repairing a dysfunctional team and helping them find ways to collaborate genuinely.

In This Step, You Have Two Tasks

1. Solidify the end result in your mind. One of these "ends" is the leader's purpose. What does the team leader hope to achieve with the workshop? Their purpose and vision for what they want will give you some idea of the type of workshop you will design.

2. Begin preparing yourself for achieving the first milestone: the 1st Draft Plan. With the client's end goal clear in your mind, you can start considering potential design elements for your workshop.

Common workshop goals or outcomes include:

- Improving an inefficient work process

- Creating a business plan

- Clarifying roles, responsibilities, and accountabilities

- Conflict resolution to improve the lack of trust and respect

Knowing the purpose of your workshop allows you to consider possible workshop tools and exercises. For example, if the team needs role clarification, you could use a complex **Responsibility Assignment Matrix** or RACI exercise.

Or, you might opt for RMT's far more straightforward version, **Defining Teammate Roles and Responsibilities Exercise Using these Four Questions**. You can find this exercise and two others in the **Resource** section of this book.

If you are serving a repeat client, you may already have some idea about what a well-designed workshop might look like for this team. That puts you ahead of the game.

But if you haven't worked with this team before, and all you're starting with is an inkling of what they want to achieve, that's okay, too. You will find out more when you meet with the team leader in Step 2 to discuss their hopes and expectations. And you'll learn all you need to know when you complete teammate interviews in Step 7.

If you follow the 12 steps outlined here, you will easily design a workshop teammates can't wait to attend.

To help you see the big picture, here are the main milestones and meetings along the way as you design and present your workshop.

Meetings

You'll have a minimum of three face-to-face meetings with the team leader:

- Step 2: Understand the Leader's Outcomes

- Step 4: Create & Present the 1st Draft Plan

- Step 8: Present the 2nd Draft Plan

Milestones

The 12 Steps Process also includes four key milestones:

- Step 4: Create & Present the 1st Draft Plan

- Step 9: Finalize Agenda, Plan, Distribute

- Step 10: Achieve First Workshop Outcomes

- Step 12: Design the Second Workshop

Preparing to Create the 1st Draft Plan

Even though you won't actually create your 1st Draft Plan until Step 4, one of your tasks in Step 1 is to start thinking about your workshop agenda and elements.

Your initial plan will include four key elements:

See Resources Section

1. **Outcomes**: Two to four statements describing the leader's desired outcomes.

2. **Agenda**: A draft of the potential exercises designed to achieve those outcomes.

3. **Punch List**: A list of potential topics, issues, challenges, or conflicts the team could address and resolve.

   a. The 1st Draft list will only include the leader's ideas.
   b. Later, the 2nd Draft Plan will include a longer Punch List based on teammate interviews' ideas.

4. **Announcement**: Here, you want to give the leader some concrete ideas on how to announce the workshop to teammates.

You will find an example called 1st Draft Team Building Plan Agenda & Punch List in the **Resources** section. You'll also find Announcing Your Workshop via Email – a Template specifically for announcement ideas.

How Long Does It Take to Design a 12 Steps RMT Workshop?

Many facilitators wonder how much preparation should go into creating a workshop. The short answer is "three to one" - three planning hours for every one hour in the workshop. For example, a two-day workshop will take up to six total days of planning.

Successful facilitators already know this ratio to be true. But if that feels daunting to you, don't worry. Just follow the steps one at a time. Your workshop will succeed, and your team will be incredibly happy with you.

· · · · ·

Now that you have the end in mind, you must get ready to meet with your team leader so you can understand their desired outcomes. We'll cover this initial meeting in Step 2.

How to Design a
Right-Minded
TEAMWORK
Team-Building Workshop:
12-Step Process

Contract
Designing
the Workshop

1 Start with the End in Mind ▼ Leader Defines Purpose

2 Leader Meets Facilitator ▼ Shares Purpose & Outcomes

3 Wants vs. Needs ▼ Facilitator Uncovers Root Causes

4 Facilitator Presents First Draft Plan to Leader

5 Leader Announces Workshop & Prepares Teammates

6 Facilitator Conducts Right-Minded Teamwork Survey

7 Facilitator Interviews All Teammates

8 Facilitator Presents Second Draft Plan to Leader

9 Leader & Facilitator Finalize Agenda & Workshop Plan

10 Achieve Workshop Outcomes

11 Track & Report Progress for the Next 90 Days

12 Leader & Facilitator Begin Designing the Second Workshop

Carry On: Continuing After the Workshop

Commence Facilitating the Workshop

Step 2 – Understand the Leader's Outcomes

All ethical counselors start their work by understanding where the client is (or where they think they are). Only then can they begin the work to move the client to where they want to be.

Guess what? As a facilitator, you must do the same with your team.

In Step 2, you'll begin to understand what the team leader thinks is happening within their team and why.

In This Step, You Have Three Tasks

1. Meet with your team leader to understand the leader's desired outcomes, including what they want to achieve from:
   a. Their overall team-building efforts
   b. The first workshop

2. Agree on a plan forward and a timeline for accomplishing the milestones.

3. Create a strong working partnership.

What's an Outcome?

Clearly written outcomes describe what will be accomplished during the workshop.

You can think of them as products, results, or deliverables that the team will produce by the workshop's end. An outcome could be a list, a plan, or a Work Agreement - something tangible the team will create.

If you contrast outcomes with goals, it's easy to see the difference.

Team goals might include "increase sales by 15%" or "reduce costs by 10%."

You can't achieve those in a meeting. But you can create a plan or establish a **Work Agreement** to support the team in achieving those goals. Make sense?

Here are a few examples of solid workshop outcomes:

- Discuss and agree on how to improve team interactions and communications
- Brainstorm and prioritize how we will enhance customer satisfaction
- Agree on the top three improvement initiatives for the next 90 Days
- Agree on roles and responsibilities for implementing the new software

IMPORTANT:

Clear workshop outcomes are the most critical element of an RMT workshop design.

Why? Because everything you do while designing and facilitating the workshop must work together to achieve those outcomes.

Preparing for Your First Meeting with the Leader

To make the most of your first meeting, there are some specific things you can do.

- Think about what you already know about the team leader's needs. What kind of pressure is the team leader under?

- Put together a short list of four to six questions to ask the leader.

- Accept that there is never enough time to discuss everything. Remember, you will have future conversations.

*See **Possible Questions to Ask in a First Team Leader Meeting** in the **Resources** section for specific examples.*

Conducting Your First Meeting with the Leader

The first meeting could take about two hours.

During the first 60-90 minutes, your goal is to understand the leader's outcomes. During the last 30 minutes, you want to propose a plan to move forward and an anticipated timeframe.

Most leaders have little difficulty saying what they want to achieve. Many desired outcomes involve removing pains or costs. Pains are irritations or frustrations, often due to constantly having to deal with poor work behavior. Costs are things that impact the bottom line, like budget cuts or the loss of a valued customer.

Pains and costs are often symptoms of dysfunctional teamwork behavior. But more on that in Step 3.

In your meeting notes, capture any desired outcomes the leader says they want to achieve. Repeat those outcomes back to them during the meeting to demonstrate you are truly hearing them. Later, when you write the 1st Draft Plan, you'll translate these notes into clearly written outcome statements.

Agree on a Plan Forward

Before you finish your meeting, make certain you have a clear discussion about the plan going forward. Don't rush this part of the process - you'll regret it if you do.

The best way to discuss an appropriate timeline is to briefly walk through the 12 Steps together and agree on milestone dates.

Using these steps will ensure you don't miss important tasks. They will also make the leader even more confident in your ability to design a successful, practical workshop.

Create a Strong Working Partnership

No two leaders are the same. And, of course, you always want to start your working relationship off on the right foot. Here are a few things to keep in mind during your first meeting.

1. Set the Tone

Your first meeting sets the tone for the rest of your relationship, including your workshop. Therefore, managing yourself well is essential from the very start.

To make a positive first impression, arrive on time, and be thoroughly prepared.

Listen to your leader's problems and offer practical suggestions and solutions. They will quickly realize you are a valued team-building partner. Their confidence in you is exactly what you want to achieve.

2. Encourage Trust and Confidence

When you interact with the leader in a genuine and caring way, you will gain a greater understanding of the team's issues.

Why? Because choosing to interact authentically encourages trust and confidence. The more the leader trusts you, the more open and honest they will be with you about their concerns.

See the **5 Keys to Proper Communication** in the **Resources** section for specific interaction ideas.

3. Be Humble (Important!!)

Your primary function is to help the leader achieve their workshop outcomes. Their success is not about you. When their workshop succeeds, it will be because the leader and teammates did their work. So be there to support them but let the leader and the team take center stage.

By the end of your first meeting with the team leader, you will:

- Understand their initial desired outcomes and overall team building goals

- Agree to follow the 12 Steps - Your team leader will love them!

- Be well on your way to creating a solid, mutually agreeable working partnership

. . . . .

In the next step, you'll make sense of all the information you learned in this first leader meeting.

How to Design a
Right-Minded
TEAMWORK
Team-Building Workshop:
12-Step Process

Step 3 – Uncovering Root Causes

What the leader wants is not always what the team needs.

In This Step, You Have Two Tasks

1. Reflect.
    a. Assume the leader's outcomes are symptoms of team dysfunction. What could be the underlying or root causes of those symptoms?

    b. Begin thinking about team exercises that will remove or transform those root causes.

2. Begin writing your first draft plan.

A (True!) Root Cause Story

An incredibly good team leader once asked me, "Can you teach my team your three-day facilitation workshop... but in two days?"

I said yes, then asked, "What specifically are you wanting to achieve? What behaviors are you looking for?"

He told me, "Our team meetings are horrible, and if everyone knew just how hard it was to facilitate them, they wouldn't be so disagreeable and hard to get along with."

I said, "Okay, how about letting me interview your teammates [Step 7], and then I'll come with a detailed plan [Step 8]?" He agreed to my proposed timeframe and plan forward.

(I opted to skip the team survey because I believed I could get enough information from the interviews.)

Taking the information I already knew, I created a 1st Draft Plan and gave it to him right away. I wanted to show him the desired outcomes for the team member interviews.

In the **Resources** section, you will find both 1st and 2nd Draft Plans. Note these are the actual 1st and 2nd plans I used with this team.

We identified the following first-draft outcomes:

- Discuss and agree on how to improve meeting effectiveness.

- Discuss and agree on how to improve team communications.

Next, I interviewed all 12 teammates, mostly engineers, and geoscientists. Unanimously, they agreed their meetings were horrible.

But unlike their leader, who felt everyone was disagreeable in meetings because they didn't appreciate how hard it was to facilitate team meetings and encourage constructive conversation, the team's view was very different.

Nearly every teammate said something like, *"Our meetings are so bad because when one person brings up a different opinion, others jump in, interrupting and arguing, and then aggressively saying things like, 'That won't work!'"*

After reflecting on the leader's initial outcomes and what I heard in the interviews, it was clear the leader's desired outcome for improvement with facilitation skill training was not the root cause of the team's challenges. The underlying problem was that this team did not know how to argue constructively. They simply weren't fighting fair.

So, I proposed the following approach for the two-day workshop.

Day 1

- Dan will teach meeting facilitation and communication skills – 2 hours.

- Teammates will discuss and agree on how they will use those skills to present contrary opinions and resolve conflicts. This discussion will lead to the creation of team Work Agreements – 2 hours.

- The team will identify current conflicts and practice using the new Work Agreements to resolve them – 4 hours.

Day 2

- The team will continue applying their Work Agreements to their specific conflicts: work ethic, customer service, and teammate roles.

The team leader loved the idea. So did his teammates. They had a remarkably successful workshop. They created three Work Agreements that, if they implemented them properly, would resolve their conflicts.

A few months later, I called the leader to inquire about how the team was functioning. He replied, "I wish I had brought you in six months earlier because not only are our meetings much better, we're making much better team decisions."

*Want another true story? Look for **Another Root Cause Story** in the **Resources** section to read about a leader who asked me to improve leadership trust and help a poor-performing partner.*

A Simple Way to Find a Root Cause

Let's use the story above as an example. What did the leader initially want? He wanted his teammates to learn how to facilitate meetings.

Now, let's reframe his desired outcome by assuming facilitation is not the true outcome but rather a symptom of his team's dysfunction.

If poor facilitation is the symptom, what causes it? Team conflict.

And what could cause a team, which works well together outside of meetings to experience team conflict while in meetings? What could be the root cause? No agreement on how to converse and argue constructively.

With the root cause identified, the solution is a Work Agreement.

In their Work Agreement, this team described how they all agreed to "argue nicely," fight fair, and engage in healthy conflict resolution during their team meetings.

Now, even when conflicts occur, the team has the tools and a mutual team Agreement to guide them and help them reach productive conclusions.

Though it wasn't what he originally asked for, the leader got what he wanted in the end. The teammates got what they wanted, too. And the team got what it needed. Success is all around.

A Mental Model for Identifying Root Causes of Conflict

Let's say you see or hear about a team conflict. You immediately assume the conflict is a symptom and start to look for a root cause.

There are three levels to consider in this model:

1. Top-level: **Whats**

High-level team elements including vision, mission, and goals

2. Mid-level: **Hows**

Processes, like roles and responsibilities; usually subsets of Whats

3. Base-level: **Relationships**

Occur between people and often focus on emotions and feelings

Identify Root Causes

What
- Vision & Mission
- Goals & Objectives
- Deliverables
- Charter

How
- Roles & Responsibilities
- Accountabilities
- Operation Plans
- Work Agreements
- Decision-Making

Relationship
- Work Styles
- Trust
- Interpersonal
- Past History
- Memories

Let's start at the base level.

Conflicts are first experienced or felt in **Relationships**.

Examples of Relationship conflicts include:
- work style clashes
- lack of trust
- poor interpersonal behavior
- negative history being dredged up

We now know most conflicts are symptoms of underlying root causes. So, if these conflicts are also symptoms, they must be caused by something else.

Most often, the "something else" that is not working is a **How**.

Examples of dysfunctional Hows include:
- lack of clear roles, responsibility, or accountability
- no clear team operating plans
- no clarity about how decisions are made
- no Work Agreements

Hows like these are often the cause of conflict in teammate relationships.

For example, if roles and responsibilities are unclear, specific teamwork tasks likely fall between the cracks. When those tasks are not completed, teammates blame others and no longer trust them to do their jobs. Only after teammates clarify roles and responsibilities can trust be rebuilt.

But sometimes roles are clear, and teammates still don't trust one another.

When that's the case, the mistrust must have a different root cause. It's time to move to the next level - the **What** - to see if the root cause lies there.

At the What level, you may discover a major disagreement within the team regarding the team's goals and objectives.

For example, if it turns out the leader strongly believes in a set of goals and objectives many teammates don't like, many teammates may lack trust in their leader.

Once you know whether your root cause exists at the How or the What level, you can suggest an effective solution. In this example, you'd suggest a vision, mission, and goals team-building workshop to correct the team's misaligned Whats.

*In the **Resources** section, **Another Root Cause Story** describes my root cause discovery of a What level problem with an architectural design firm - and our subsequent team building workshop to address the issue.*

Many root causes behind team dysfunction and conflict exist at either the How level or the What level. But occasionally, root causes go deeper still.

Let's say the Whats and Hows are all in place, and all team members agree they are functional, but trust is still absent. If that's the case, the root cause may actually lie at the level of individual **Relationships**.

If that is the case, you, as the facilitator, will need to work with the leader to identify and individually coach teammates who are experiencing a lack of trust.

Address Root Causes, Not Symptoms

IMPORTANT: Right-Minded Teamwork is about resolving root cause issues, not addressing symptoms.

Team building approaches that do not tackle root causes often backfire. If you missed it, see the section *From Worst to Best: Team-Building Exercises* at the beginning of this book on this topic. They may cause teams to falter or fall short of goals. They can even fuel the real issue behind the team's dysfunction instead of resolving it.

In our example, the well-meaning leader who asked if I could do a three-day workshop in two days came to me thinking he needed a training class. But if I had simply done what he asked, the team would have received unhelpful information, and the leader would still be struggling with the same issue. I would have failed both the team and the leader.

Instead, by looking for the root cause first, we ended up designing and executing a practical Right-Minded Teamwork workshop. We solved the underlying problem and delivered the leader's desired result... even though it wasn't what the leader initially asked for.

For this reason, it's best never to assume team leaders know the real problem. Many times, they are right, but before moving ahead, always verify the team leader's opinions using RMT surveys and teammate interviews.

You may be wondering whether it is okay to tell your team leader, "You're not always right."

The answer is, in short, yes.

Using your best communication skills, you can let the leader know that you must incorporate all teammate ideas into the final agenda while you will start the design process with their outcomes in mind.

Remember, as a facilitator; you are primarily responsible for helping the team find and resolve root causes. It would be best if you had everybody's input to make that happen.

You can say something like, *"I'm sure you will agree that none of us is as smart as all of us, so it will be far better to have all team members' design input. It will create genuine excitement for achieving the workshop outcomes, rather than the resistance we might receive if we just design something without their input."*

With that said, if your team leader does not allow you to interview teammates and take the team's perspective into account, run the other way!

Do not facilitate the session. Politely explain that you are committed to Right-Minded Teamwork principles. You would not be acting in integrity if you did not adequately prepare.

Begin Writing the 1st Draft Plan

Did you forget we're still in Step 3 of the 12 Steps to Design a Right-Minded Teamwork Team Building Workshop? Let's get back to it.

Now that you've uncovered root causes, it's time to make sense of what your team leader shared. Give yourself several days to complete this step. During this time, you might even call the leader to test a strategy or ask for clarification.

Once you feel clear, it's time to begin putting your plan together.

To get started, simply start writing. Your 1st Draft doesn't have to be comprehensive, but it must accurately reflect what the leader thinks they want.

You can use the 1st Draft Team-Building Workshop Plan Agenda & Punch List in the Resources section as a guide.

Remember, your 1st Draft doesn't have to be perfect. You have until Step 9 to solidify your workshop outcomes. That means the outcomes discussion between you, the leader, and the teammates can evolve between now and then.

Let it be a natural process where you gradually add, edit, and even postpone some outcomes to address in future workshops.

At this point, you'll also want to give some thought as to how you will present your plan to the leader. You could email it the day before your meeting, or you could show up and present it. Which will suit your team leader better?

· · · · ·

You've reflected. You've started writing your plan. You're now ready for Step 4: Time to finish the plan and present it.

How to Design a
Right-Minded
TEAMWORK
Team-Building Workshop:
12-Step Process

Step 4 – Create & Present the 1st Draft Plan

Presenting the 1st Draft Plan is your opportunity to show your team leader you've been listening carefully and that you understand what they want to accomplish within their team.

In This Step, You Have Three Tasks

1. Finalize your 1st Draft Plan.

2. Present, clarify, and modify the Plan.

3. Agree on how and when to announce the workshop.

Finalizing the 1st Draft Plan

Your 1st Draft Plan must contain four key elements:

1. Outcomes
2. Agenda
3. Punch List
4. Announcement

Let's go through each element individually.

Outcomes: 2-4 Statements

First, you'll write out descriptions that reflect the leader's desired outcomes.

The most practical outcome for a Right-Minded Teamwork workshop is a Work Agreement.

Nine times out of ten, a Work Agreement of some kind will be the best outcome for what the team needs.

Work Agreements:

- Are created jointly by all teammates and the team leader.

- Define how teammates will work together to resolve, eventually, all their Punch List issues.

When you hear about issues and needs like the ones in the Root Cause Story from Step 3, it's easy to see how creating Work Agreements makes practical sense.

However, a cautionary note: Work Agreements are so incredibly simple that some people are quick to dismiss the concept as too elementary. When teammates think this way, they bog the team down with unnecessary complexity and confusion. These teammates can sabotage the team-building workshop.

Sometimes even team leaders can be skeptics. If you encounter this, do your best to present the practicality and usefulness of Work Agreements. Don't give up, and don't give in to the argument that Work Agreements won't work. They will - when teammates live them.

Of course, if they don't live them, the teammates fail. The Agreements did not fail.

Preemptively, when you present your plan, you can also say something like, *"I hear you want better meetings and better communication. I believe both topics can be successfully addressed by following a mutually agreed-upon Work Agreement.*

"Let's do this. I will complete the team interviews, and afterward, I'll propose a 2nd Draft Plan. In the meantime, let's assume that Work Agreements will successfully address and resolve meetings and communication. How does that sound to you?"

Because you come across confident that a team with solid Work Agreements will indeed achieve their workshop outcomes, your team leader will likely agree.

Facilitating Team Work Agreements

During your workshop, it is likely you will be creating Work Agreements. As you practice RMT with more and more clients, creating these Agreements will become second nature to you.

At first, though, you may find it helpful to know the specific steps to follow to create effective Work Agreements for any team.

In the **Resources** section, you will find **Work Agreements: A Narrative Description** of the 10 Facilitation Steps.

 To Learn More…

To learn how to facilitate work agreements, go to RightMindedTeamwork.com or your favorite book retailer and pick up your copy ***How to Facilitate Team Work Agreements:*** *A Practical, 10-Step Process for Building a Right-Minded Team That Works as One.*

Agenda

This is only your 1st Draft, so you don't need a detailed agenda right now. Just aim to present a general flow of agenda items.

*Let's continue to use the Root Cause Story's **1st Draft Plan** as your template. You can find it in the **Resources** section of this book.*

In the template agenda, you will see that the leader welcomes and

See Resources Section

kicks off the meeting, followed by a discussion on what effective meetings and communication look like.

After that, you will see placeholders for the team's Punch List issues. And, at the end, you will wrap up and close the workshop.

Completing this template will give you a strong first draft agenda.

Punch List

The Punch List is a list of teamwork topics for the team to address and resolve.

The list you present in your 1st Draft will only include the leader's outcome ideas, but the 2nd Draft will be longer because it will also contain teammate ideas collected during your teammate interviews.

Announcement

The final element of the 1st Draft Plan is determining how and when to announce the workshop.

The ideal way to announce the workshop is in a team meeting. If that's not possible, an email invitation will suffice. We will discuss the actual announcement in more detail in Step 5.

Presenting & Discussing Your 1st Draft Plan

Once your 1st Draft Plan is complete, you are ready to present it to your team leader.

Presenting this Plan is usually straightforward and non-threatening because the 1st Draft reflects what the leader wants.

Presenting the 2nd Draft Plan can be more challenging because items you present in the updated Punch List might be difficult for the leader to hear based on the teammate interviews.

Just remember, if you follow these steps and continue to keep the leader informed as you interview teammates, you will easily help the leader embrace difficult feedback.

To present your 1st Draft Plan, set a meeting with your team leader, and bring your ideas in writing.

Don't use a PowerPoint presentation. It is too impersonal for this one-on-one meeting with your team leader. Remember, the 1st Draft template is an excellent example of what to present and how much information to include.

When presenting, sit next to the leader rather than across from them. Walk them through each page and each item. They will ask clarifying questions. Spend as much time as necessary to answer each question.

I guarantee the leader will think of several terrific ideas on how to modify and improve your plan. Be grateful for this input. Remember, you are partners.

Take notes on their suggestions. Write down their ideas. Make sure they see you do that. Then, be sure to incorporate their ideas into your 2nd Draft Plan.

Other Topics to Briefly Discuss

There are several other topics you should make a point to cover during the 1st Draft Plan meeting:

1.   The Final Decision

Even though everyone will contribute to the workshop design, the leader must understand they have the ultimate authority to approve the workshop agenda.

2.   The Design Team

If you have worked with this team before, ask if two teammates might work with you as a design team. This is the beginning of transferring workshop development responsibility to the team.

3.   Read Right-Minded Teamwork?

Decide if teammates will read our book ***Right-Minded Teamwork***: *9 Right Choices for Building a Team That Works as One* in advance of the workshop.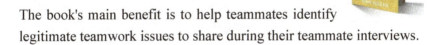

The book's main benefit is to help teammates identify legitimate teamwork issues to share during their teammate interviews.

4. Conduct RMT Survey

There are two good two reasons to survey your team:

- It helps the team pinpoint workshop outcomes.

- Surveying is an excellent way to track actual teamwork progress.

I recommend surveying the team every three months and showcasing results on a scorecard. Doing so helps reinforce positive gains and points out any downward trends before they become toxic.

5. Teammate Preparation

What will be your initial message to the team? In the 1st Draft Plan meeting with your team leader, your task is only to present a few initial ideas and get feedback. For example, in the Root Cause Story, the initial idea was to simply ask teammates to offer suggestions for improving meetings and communication.

You'll learn more about teammate preparation in the next step.

6. Teammate Interviews

Discuss logistics on when and where you will conduct these interviews. You may want to agree on two or three standard questions to ask. At a minimum, you will show teammates the leader's outcomes and ask if they agree. You may also ask if they have other issues to propose.

7. Preventions and Interventions

Ask the team leader if any issues could prevent teammates from achieving the desired outcomes.

For example, one issue might be a teammate who is resistant to team building because he hasn't seen it work very well in the past.

Confirm your leader is willing to work with you to overcome these challenges. Your discussion will enable you to create and implement preventions that will, hopefully, prevent those issues from happening.

Also, discuss what you will do if your preventions don't work, and a teammate continues to be resistant. How will you intervene? Your pre-planned intervention could be that you and the leader will talk privately with the teammate during a break.

Continue to discuss preventions and interventions with the leader all the way up to the day of the workshop.

In Step 9, we will discuss this fundamental planning process more thoroughly.

8. Looking Ahead

Inform the leader that there will soon come a time (around Step 8) where you will discuss other workshop design elements, such as:

- team-building roles and responsibilities

- how to track team progress

- when to conduct the second workshop

If you are a new team-building facilitator, all these tasks may seem a bit overwhelming. While there are numerous things to consider, they will make perfect sense once you've followed them a few times.

For the more experienced facilitator, you will be happy all these tasks are clearly presented for you and your team leader to use right now.

Don't forget your special function I mentioned in this book's Preface. You are there to help them to create and sustain Right-Minded Teamwork, which is how you are doing your part to make the world a better place for all.

. . . . .

Now that the presentation of the 1st Draft Plan is behind you, and you've gotten plenty of feedback from your team leader, it's time for Step 5.

How to Design a
Right-Minded
TEAMWORK
Team-Building Workshop:
12-Step Process

Contract:
Designing
the Workshop

1 Start with the
End in Mind
▼
Leader
Defines
Purpose

2 Leader Meets
Facilitator
▼
Shares
Purpose
&
Outcomes

3 Wants vs. Needs
▼
Facilitator
Uncovers
Root Causes

4 Facilitator Presents
First Draft
Plan to Leader

5 Leader Announces
Workshop &
Prepares
Teammates

6 Facilitator
Conducts
Right-Minded
Teamwork
Survey

7 Facilitator
Interviews
All
Teammates

8 Facilitator
Presents
Second Draft
Plan
to Leader

9 Leader &
Facilitator
Finalize Agenda
&
Workshop
Plan

Commence:
Facilitating
the
Workshop

10 Achieve
Workshop
Outcomes

Carry On:
Continuing
After the
Workshop

11 Track & Report
Progress for
the Next 90 Days

12 Leader &
Facilitator
Begin Designing
the
Second
Workshop

Step 5 – Announce the Workshop & Prepare Teammates

With a solid 1st Draft Plan in place, you're ready to engage the team in the workshop planning process.

In This Step, You Have Two Tasks

1. Announce the workshop.

2. Start preparing teammates.

Announcing the Workshop

The best possible way to announce the workshop is in a team meeting. If that's not possible, the leader can send an email invitation to all team members. Either way, it is your responsibility to create the "talking points" for the leader's announcement.

Caution:

Do not ask teammates to "buy into" this team-building workshop because this 12-step method does not need you to ask such a silly question. Since you will invite all teammates to help design the workshop outcomes and agenda, they will automatically "buy-in," thus creating acceptance and accountability. For more on this, listen to the online training class video for this Step 5.

Announcing in a Team Meeting

Ideally, in a team meeting where all teammates are present, the leader announces the workshop. They present the purpose and possible outcomes. And they introduce you.

Teammates can ask clarifying questions; the leader's answers will show how the workshop results will benefit teammates and the team's customers. This will create genuine excitement for the workshop.

The leader will communicate that this will be a custom-designed workshop where the team will achieve real-world results. You will be dealing with the team's actual work issues.

The leader will also communicate preparation assignments, such as:
- Reading **Right-Minded Teamwork**: *9 Right Choices for Building a Team That Works as One*
- Taking the RMT teammate survey
- Making interview arrangements

Announcing via Email

If the leader must email the workshop announcement, it is your responsibility to draft the text.

Caution:

A poorly communicated announcement can create resistance. Take time to craft your message. Choose your words carefully and frame this team-building effort as a positive benefit for all.

*In the **Resources** section, use the **Announcing the Workshop via Email - a Template.***

Preparing Teammates

Leaders love hearing teammates must do their part to prepare for the workshop.

You can say something like:

It's crucial we make sure the teammates are ready for the workshop. They must be prepared to discuss and agree on how to resolve their Punch List items. That means two things:

1. *We want to allow them to help design the Punch List and workshop outcomes.*

2. *We also want them to be ready to offer legitimate solutions at the beginning of the workshop.*

There's no question the leader will wholeheartedly agree!

There are two steps involved in preparing teammates.

Manage Teammate Expectations

Let teammates know what they can expect to happen before the workshop by communicating the following key points:

- **Planning**: Let teammates know the leader wants them all to contribute to and influence the workshop agenda.

- **Survey**: Ask them to complete a questionnaire that will help identify the most critical workshop outcomes. Let them know how and when the survey will be conducted.

- **Logistics**: Make sure they know the dates and location of the workshop.

- **Reading**: Ask teammates to read *Right-Minded Teamwork: 9 Right Choices for Building a Team That Works as One* and let them know why it will be helpful.

- **Interviews**: Inform them that the facilitator will interview each team member and that the team leader encourages honesty. Let them know interviews will last 30-60 minutes.

- **Final Workshop Agenda**: Say to them that you will use the survey and interview feedback to create a final agenda and Punch List for the team that you will distribute in advance of the workshop.

Inform Teammates How to Prepare

Workshop preparation should not take teammates more than 30 minutes to complete.

Be sure your instructions are simple, straightforward, and valuable.

In the Root Cause Story in Step 3, I asked teammates to come prepared to offer solutions to their unresolved conflicts.

You will write the specific preparation instructions after you finalize the workshop outcomes in Step 9. Still, sometimes, you already know you're going to ask certain team members to research a topic and present their findings at this early design stage.

If you know any preparation tasks that need to be achieved before the workshop, go ahead and give those assignments now instead of waiting until Step 9. For example, I once had a team leader who had to secure a legal opinion before conducting the workshop. In another team, we sent several teammates off to shop for a sophisticated software program.

. . . . .

With the workshop announced and team members gearing up, it's time to focus on your next significant milestone: finalizing the workshop design. That starts with Step 6, conducting the RMT survey.

How to Design a
Right-Minded
TEAMWORK
Team-Building Workshop:
12-Step Process

Contract:
Designing
the Workshop

1 Start with the End in Mind ▼ Leader Defines Purpose

2 Leader Meets Facilitator ▼ Shares Purpose & Outcomes

3 Wants vs. Needs ▼ Facilitator Uncovers Root Causes

4 Facilitator Presents First Draft Plan to Leader

5 Leader Announces Workshop & Prepares Teammates

6 Facilitator Conducts Right-Minded Teamwork Survey

7 Facilitator Interviews All Teammates

8 Facilitator Presents Second Draft Plan to Leader

9 Leader & Facilitator Finalize Agenda & Workshop Plan

Commence Facilitating the Workshop

10 Achieve Workshop Outcomes

Carry On: Continuing After the Workshop

11 Track & Report Progress for the Next 90 Days

12 Leader & Facilitator Begin Designing the Second Workshop

Step 6 – Conduct the
Right-Minded Teammate Survey

Steps 6-9 combine the following four steps into one more significant step that ultimately leads to finalizing the workshop design. How and when you complete these steps is up to you and the team leader. Just note that all four steps contribute to the end design.

In Step 6, we'll be conducting the RMT survey.

In This Step, You Have Two Tasks

1. Decide whether you will use a teammate survey.

2. Administer, analyze, and use the survey summary results to identify workshop outcomes.

Why Use a Right-Minded Teamwork Survey?

There are two excellent reasons for using a survey:

1. A survey allows team members to individually and collectively identify the best workshop outcomes to address in the workshop.

2. When conducted every three months, the RMT survey becomes an excellent scorecard for tracking actual teamwork progress. Summary results help reinforce positive teamwork gains and reveal negative trends before they become toxic.

Choosing Your Survey

There are two available Right-Minded Teamwork surveys and one Team Assessment.

1. RMT's **9 Right Choices Survey**
2. RMT's 20-Question **Team Perception Survey**
3. RMT's **Team Performance Factor Assessment**

The first two are anonymous surveys, and the third one is an assessment we used in RMT's 4th Element – Team Operating System.

Let's take a closer look at each.

RMT's 9 Right Choices Survey

The 9 Right Choices Survey is a nine-question perception survey. It aligns with the nine choices presented in the Right-Minded Teamwork book.

The survey is below, and you may download a FREE copy of it at RightMindedTeamwork.com. Search for *Utilize the 9 Teammate Questions to Track Your Team's Performance.*

The simplest and fastest way to conduct the 9 Right Choices Survey is in a team meeting, where you'll simply ask team members to complete their questionnaires and turn them in to the facilitator.

If you announce the workshop in a whole team meeting in Step 5, you can conduct the survey right then.

Also, ask teammates to provide constructive, written comments that help clarify survey scores and make it easier to identify the best outcomes to address in the next workshop.

When administering the survey, let teammates know everyone will receive a copy of the summary results.

9 Right Choice Questions

	No 1	2	Yes 3
1. Has our team consciously made a choice to follow Right-Minded principles?			
2. Do all teammates act and behave as one united team?			
3. Do all teammates communicate their thoughts, opinions, and ideas in effective and appropriate ways?			
4. Do all teammates understand, agree, and actively support the team's vision?			
5. Has our team developed effective and practical Work Agreements that will help us achieve the team's vision?			
6. Does our team focus on completing the agreed-upon critical-few work processes and not get drawn into the trivial-many?			
7. Do we always look for ways to correct mistakes and improve our team's business performance and relationships?			
8. Are all conflicts effectively addressed and resolved in a timely and humanistic manner?			
9. Do all teammates feel they are appropriately acknowledged and recognized for their job contributions?			
Comments: What should teammates Start, Stop or Continue doing?			

Analyzing and Using Survey Results

The RMT 9 Right Choices Survey is a "pulse" survey designed to measure the team's collective perception of their current state. It is pretty simple to administer and analyze, making it highly worthwhile.

When you are ready to analyze survey results, there are three tiers of possible performance, no matter your team's size.

If your **Average Team Member Score** is:

15 or less: Your team is functioning far below potential.

16–22: Your team is doing okay but is still working below potential.

23–27: Your team is doing fine, but you must agree on how to keep it that way.

As for teammate comments, you will want to organize them by creating groups of similar remarks.

If many team members are saying the same thing, you have found a common issue; it is likely a team-building issue to address in the workshop. Please include it in the Punch List.

You'll also want to look for any comments that validate the leader's outcomes.

Use your survey data and analysis to plan teammate interviews. You might ask teammates questions or invite discussion around common survey themes. You might also ask questions about any potential new outcomes that popped up in the survey.

Calculating and Summarizing Survey Results

To calculate results, first, tally the scores for each column. Then divide your overall score by the number of teammates to determine the average score.

EXAMPLE: Eight teammates completed the survey.
For question #1, four teammates gave it a 1, three scored 2, and only one person said 3.

Total Team Scores	No 1	2	Yes 3
1. ...follow Right-Minded principles?	4	3	1
2. ...one united team?	3	5	
3. ...communicate in appropriate ways?	2	4	2
4. ...support the team's vision?	3	5	
5. ...practical Work Agreements?	4	2	2
6. ...critical-few work processes?	5	3	
7. ...correct mistakes?	3	4	1
8. ...resolve conflicts?	5	2	1
9. ...recognize job contributions?	5	3	
Subtotal	34	31	7

Calculating the Average Team Member Score

No = 1	34 x 1 =	34
2	31 x 2 =	62
Yes = 3	7 x 3 =	21
	Total numerical score	117
Overall Average Score	117 / 8 =	14.625

RMT's 20-Question Team Perception Survey

If you want a more comprehensive survey, the 20-Question Team Perception Survey (TPS) is an excellent choice. I used it for three decades with clients and found teams that used it consistently were more successful as a result.

*For example, in the **Resources** section, look for **Work Agreements Bring People Together as One,** to find a team who used their TPS results to create Work Agreements. After one year of following these Agreements, survey results showed they'd improved their overall teammate trust score by 78%, which only motivated them more.

As with the RMT 9 Right Choices Survey, the Team Perception Survey is not a predictive tool. Instead, it summarizes teammate's perceptions of their team's current situation.

Perceptions are important. After all, isn't it true that teammate perceptions are their reality? And isn't it true they react and behave according to their perceived reality? Therein lies the value of both the 9 Right Choices Survey and the 20-Question Team Perception Survey.

The TPS questions are basic yet holistic, simple yet complete. Together, they represent a balanced set of variables, the full range of core competencies necessary for becoming a high-performing team.

To make your assessment even more relevant to a specific team, the TPS questions are easily customizable. If a concept (such as work process, business plan, safety, or risk-taking) is not clear enough, you can simply edit the questionnaire to meet the team's needs.

The TPS is meant to be anonymous and confidential, but it's not unusual for people to acknowledge their identity in the comments section. Teams that liberally use the comment section are often the teams that gain the most from their TPS.

Just like the 9 Right Choices Survey, the real benefit of the 20-Question TPS is not in the data. It is in the team dialogues about the data and the shifts in perception and behavior that result from those discussions.

Common results from TPS dialogues include:
- Clearer vision, mission, and objectives
- A clearer understanding of work processes, like roles and responsibilities
- Improved interpersonal dynamics, such as increased trust, respect, safety, and willingness to speak up without fear of retaliation

 To Learn More…

To learn more about the **Team Perception Survey**, go to RightMindedTeamwork.com and search for Team Perception Survey.

Team Performance Factor Assessment

The Team Operating System is a six-step, 90-day, continuous improvement operating system that organizes your team functions to increase the likelihood of achieving customer satisfaction.

The system includes the *Team Performance Factor Assessment*, which you will use to help teammates identify two to three improvement opportunities every 90 days.

The 25 performance factors in this assessment (the third step in the system) are perfectly aligned with and thus effectively measure the six steps of your operating system. They measure all aspects of Right-Minded Teamwork.

 To Learn More...

To learn more about the **Team Performance Factor Assessment**, go to RightMindedTeamwork.com or your favorite book retailer and pick up your copy of **Right-Minded Teamwork in Any Team**: *The Ultimate Method to Create a Team That Works as One* and look for Element #4 – Team Operating System.

. . . . .

You've administered your survey, and the results are in. Now that you have the leader's outcomes and the survey results, you're ready to interview teammates - Step 7.

How to Design a
Right-Minded
TEAMWORK
Team-Building Workshop:
12-Step Process

Contract,
Designing
the Workshop

1 Start with the
End in Mind
▼
Leader
Defines
Purpose

2 Leader Meets
Facilitator
▼
Shares
Purpose
&
Outcomes

Wants vs. Needs
▼
Facilitator
Uncovers
Root Causes 3

Facilitator Presents
First Draft
Plan to Leader 4

Leader Announces
Workshop &
Prepares
Teammates

5 Facilitator
Conducts
Right-Minded
Teamwork
Survey

6 Facilitator
Interviews
All
Teammates

Facilitator
Presents
Second Draft
Plan
to Leader 8

Facilitator
Presents
Second Draft
Plan
to Leader

7

9 Leader &
Facilitator
Finalize Agenda
&
Workshop
Plan

Commence:
Facilitating
the
Workshop

10 Achieve
Workshop
Outcomes

Carry On:
Continuing
After the
Workshop

11 Track & Report
Progress for
the Next 90 Days

12 Leader &
Facilitator
Begin Designing
the
Second
Workshop

Step 7 – Facilitator Interviews All Teammates

With your survey summary in hand, it's time to dig a little deeper by interviewing individual teammates.

In This Step, You Have Three Tasks

1. Interview all teammates.

2. Create the team's Punch List.

3. Identify other potential workshop outcomes.

Yes, Interviews Take Time - They're Worth It

To design a successful RMT workshop, you must thoroughly understand what the teammates collectively believe. Interviewing is by far the best way to put this picture together.

Whatever *you* may think of the teammates right now doesn't matter.

What matters is what *they think of themselves*.

To truly help the team, you must first understand where they think they are. Knowing how *they view themselves* allows you to create the pathway to take them *where they want to be*.

Their collective answers highlight the team's strengths and flaws.

From the information you collect in this step, you will create and present more potential workshop outcomes in your 2nd Draft Plan. You will also propose exercises that reinforce their strengths and mitigate their flaws. You will find three exercises in the **Resources** section.

Becoming an Excellent Interviewer

As you become a more effective interviewer, you will see how teammate interviews can teach you everything you need to know about designing and facilitating that team's workshop.

But you won't start as an expert, so be willing to practice and learn. You can test-drive your interviewing skills in almost any conversation.

Interviewing Tips

- Interview all teammates and always interview one person at a time.

- Spread your interviews out over several days.

- Let each person know everyone's answers will be summarized in a Punch List, without attributing as to who said what. Everyone on the team will receive a copy.

- Share the leader's suggested outcomes and ask what the teammate thinks of them.

- Ask what they think of the survey's common themes.

- Ask which outcomes they believe should be achieved in the workshop and which ones could be addressed in future workshops.

- Ask, "What would cause this workshop to fail?"

- Remember, you are looking for root causes, not just symptoms.

You'll start formulating your 2nd Draft Plan ideas as soon as you complete your first interview. It's okay to start testing some of your ideas in later teammate interviews.

Want more interview questions? Look for **More Facilitator Interview Questions** *in the Resources section.*

Punch List

The Punch List is a list of teamwork topics that this team wants to address and resolve in their workshop.

You will finalize the Punch List after your last interview. It contains the evidence you'll use to design the 2nd Draft Plan.

See Resources Section

To write a good Punch List:

- Devote two to three hours of uninterrupted time.

- Re-read all your individual interview notes.

- Relive those conversations in your mind.

- Dig deeper.

- Uncover more root causes.

If two or more teammates suggest a topic, make sure to include it, but do not attribute teammate names to issues.

Write Punch List Items as Questions

When writing your Punch List, it's more effective to present the topics as questions.

Why? Because it helps **create mutual accountability**.

Let me elaborate.

If you recall the Root Cause Story in Step 3, the leader initially asked me for a straightforward two-day team training class. But the interviews identified several unresolved conflicts that dealt with trust, respect, following through on job tasks, and work quality.

After the interviews, we decided to provide just a few hours of training at the beginning of the workshop. Then, as a team, we would apply that training to create new Work Agreements to address and resolve the team's work ethic conflicts.

Here's how I used the Punch List in that situation. In the 2nd Draft Plan, I presented to the leader, I included "Work Ethic" as an issue/topic.

The first topic under "Work Ethic" read:

1. Is it okay to have an unresolved conflict if it affects individual and/or team productivity? If not, what is our Work Agreement with respect to solving conflicts and/or giving performance feedback?

B. Work Ethic	This topic is about team interaction style, conflict resolution, work quality, productivity, interdependency, etc. that increases trust, respect, and confidence in one another.
	1. Is it okay to have an unresolved conflict if it affects individual and/or team productivity? If not, what is our Work Agreement with respect to solving conflicts and/or giving performance feedback? For instance, ...
	2. If someone doesn't do what they said they'd do (or are assigned to do), how do we call them out in a supportive way? How do we hold them accountable?
	3. If a teammate doesn't perform like you believe they should, what should you do? For example, if you believe a particular responsibility should be performed by another person, is it okay to call it out?
	4. Trust and respect: If you do not trust another person and it affects your performance, what should you do?
	5. If we feel we are not getting acknowledged/recognized for the work we're doing, what should we do?

Do you see the impact of posing the topic as a question?

By asking, *"is it okay?"* can you imagine how teammates will answer?

Will they tell you their unresolved conflict is acceptable? Will they try to convince you they should keep their disputes?

Of course not.

That's why posing workshop topics as questions is an effective way of getting everyone on board and in alignment without ever explicitly asking them.

By writing your Punch List items as questions, you encourage your team to accept responsibility and create accountability for each item on the list. When teammates agree there is an issue and declare they want to make a Work Agreement to solve the problem, they accept accountability.

Another benefit of this approach is that neither the team leader nor facilitator have to say to teammates, "we need to get your buy-in." You never want to use that term because it implies it's your agenda and not theirs.

Discover Other Team Building Workshop Outcomes

As you write and edit your Punch List, you will naturally begin to identify other potential workshop outcomes.

In the Root Cause Story in Step 3, I started the interviews with two outcomes. After the interviews, I proposed two additional outcomes, which added to my Punch List, and ultimately, I presented in the 2nd Draft Plan.

. . . . .

In the next step, you'll use your Punch List to create and present your 2nd Draft Plan.

How to Design a
Right-Minded
TEAMWORK
Team-Building Workshop:
12-Step Process

Contract:
Designing
the Workshop

1 Start with the End in Mind ▼ Leader Defines Purpose

2 Leader Meets Facilitator ▼ Shares Purpose & Outcomes

3 Wants vs. Needs ▼ Facilitator Uncovers Root Causes

4 Facilitator Presents First Draft Plan to Leader

5 Leader Announces Workshop & Prepares Teammates

6 Facilitator Conducts Right-Minded Teamwork Survey

7 Facilitator Interviews All Teammates

8 Facilitator Presents Second Draft Plan to Leader

9 Leader & Facilitator Finalize Agenda & Workshop Plan

Commence: Facilitating the Workshop

10 Achieve Workshop Outcomes

Carry On: Continuing After the Workshop

11 Track & Report Progress for the Next 90 Days

12 Leader & Facilitator Begin Designing the Second Workshop

Step 8 – Create and Present the 2nd Draft Plan

You've surveyed the team, summarized results, interviewed all teammates, and have finalized your Punch List. Now it's time to put it all together.

In This Step, You Have Two Tasks

1. Create the 2nd Draft Plan.
2. Present and modify the Plan.

Create Your 2nd Draft Plan

After completing the first few interviews, you will naturally begin formulating your 2nd Draft Plan. Once your interviews and Punch List are complete, you have everything you need to write the detailed Plan.

Begin by reviewing the Punch List and the leader's outcomes. As you do, ask yourself:

- What team issues are preventing Right-Minded Teamwork?

- Which issues need the most immediate attention?

- Which issues should be addressed first?

- If any one issue is resolved, will it automatically resolve other issues?

With these answers in mind, it's time to revisit your workshop outcomes from your 1st Draft Plan.

At this point, you will likely have too many outcomes for the first workshop. Go ahead and recommend a long-range plan that could include more workshops.

Now, with the refined set of outcomes you think should be accomplished in the first workshop, create a 2nd Draft agenda, including facilitated exercises to ensure the team makes plans or Work Agreements to achieve their outcomes.

Then set up a meeting with your team leader to share your Plan.

Present & Modify the 2nd Draft Plan

Just like you did in Step 4, make a point to sit next to the leader as you present your 2nd Draft Plan.

This should be a "no surprise" presentation because you've kept the leader in the loop during the interviewing and surveying process.

During the meeting, walk through the 2nd Draft Plan, and discuss each outcome and its benefits.

Point out the associated agenda items, explaining how each discussion or activity supports achieving the outcomes.

As before, I guarantee your team leader will have good ideas on modifying, adding to, or even delaying parts of your plan. Welcome their feedback.

No matter what specifics come up in the 2nd Draft Plan presentation, which could last 60-90 minutes, remember the primary purpose of this meeting is to agree on the entire plan.

Once you've reached an agreement, tell the team leader, *"I will go ahead and make all the changes we've discussed. Then, I'll email the Plan to you for final approval. At that point, we will be ready to distribute the final workshop agenda."*

Additional Goals for the Second Draft Plan Meeting

In addition to agreeing on the details of the 2nd Draft Plan, there are a few other points to cover in the 2nd Draft Plan meeting.

Decide Roles & Responsibilities

At a basic level, talk to your team leader about your roles in the workshop, other than the facilitator. Explain that you may "switch hats" to speak from a trainer's perspective or share your opinion as a consultant.

Also, clarify the leader's workshop role.

During the workshop, leaders usually want to be treated like an equal, not the boss. However, they are still responsible for deciding if the team can't come to a consensus.

*In the **Resources** section, you will find a great list of **Roles & Responsibilities** you can use to support this conversation.*

Agree on Agenda Distribution

The leader should distribute the final agenda, but it is your responsibility to draft that email once again.

In your agenda announcement message, make a point to include:

- An explanation of the outcomes and agenda

- Specific teammate preparation instructions

- Confirmation of logistics (location, dates, start/end times, etc.)

Discuss "Carrying On" after the Workshop

Agree on these two post-workshop tasks:

1. "Carrying on," which means using the team's Work Agreement after the workshop.

2. Creating and using a simple method to track post-workshop team performance (a consistent team survey is an excellent example).

. . . . .

Once you and the leader are clear and aligned on the final workshop design, it's time for Step 9.

How to Design a
Right-Minded
TEAMWORK
Team-Building Workshop:
12-Step Process

Step 9 – Finalize Workshop Plan & Distribute Materials

With your team leader's stamp of approval, it's time to distribute the workshop agenda and materials.

It's also time to dig into one of the most important facilitation skills: preventions and interventions.

In This Step, You Have Two Tasks

1. Update all workshop materials based on the design your team leader has approved and distribute to teammates.

2. Look ahead. Create a plan to prevent potential problems and clarify how to intervene if they happen.

Update Materials & Distribute to the Team

Based on your approved workshop design, you'll finalize, edit, and update all workshop materials, which should include:

- Outcomes & Agenda

- Punch List

- Teammate Preparation Instructions

- Logistics (dates, place, start/end times, etc.)

The ideal way to distribute workshop materials is in an entire team meeting. If that is not possible, they should be emailed at least one week before the workshop.

IMPORTANT: Be *"kindly"* insistent that teammates ask clarifying questions before the workshop if their preparation responsibilities are not clear.

Preventions & Interventions

Before the workshop, you and the team leader must identify issues that could inhibit teammates from creating strong Work Agreements.

That discussion will lead you both to create preventions that will, hopefully, prevent those issues from happening.

However, if your preventions don't work, you also need to agree on how you will intervene.

For example, let's say there is a resistant teammate who doesn't like team building because of several bad experiences.

As a prevention, you will actively engage that teammate in designing the workshop. Hopefully, they will offer good ideas that you can incorporate into the plan. When they see their opinions have made it into the final list, they will feel validated and heard. Often, this recognition naturally leads to engagement. When it does, the prevention of engaging the resistant teammate into the design process can be deemed effective.

If the teammate does not engage or becomes resistant during the workshop, the pre-planned intervention might be for you and the leader to talk privately with the teammate during a break.

First, you and the leader need to identify potential workshop barriers. Afterward, you will create preventions and interventions for those you deem most likely to happen.

Identify Workshop Barriers

On any team, two types of barriers may arise during a workshop:
1. Process barriers
2. People barriers

Depending on the team and the barrier, these barriers can show up as minor nuisances or significant problems.

Examples of process barriers:

- An interdependent virtual team is divided into four time zones.
- Because of shift work, not all teammates can attend the workshop.
- Too many layers of management approval slow down processing.

Examples of people barriers:

- The team struggles with language or cultural differences.
- A teammate resists team building.
- There is toxic and unresolved conflict between teammates.

Most workshops have around 3-5 barriers. As you consider your team's barriers, remember your team leader knows their teammates better than you do.

Ask the leader:

- What could go wrong in the workshop?
- How can we prevent those wrongs/barriers from happening?
- How will we intervene if they happen?

This conversation often starts way back in Step 2 when you learn about the leader's desired outcomes.

When the workshop agenda is complete in Step 9, you and the leader need to finish planning your preventions and interventions. For each barrier you identify, you two will create a prevention and intervention plan.

Create a Prevention Plan

Two examples of preventative measures you can take to address a resistant teammate are: **inclusion** and a **pre-workshop agreement**.

In the planning phase, **inclusion means** you will genuinely interview the opposing teammate, ensuring that teammate knows their workshop design ideas are equally as crucial as their fellow teammates.

Share with them that it is essential all teammates, including them, believe the final workshop outcomes are worthwhile. Every teammate must be committed to achieving them for the team to succeed.

After the team leader approves the final agenda, inclusion means returning to the resistant teammate and walking through the agenda with them. Your goal is to give them a chance to get on board and embrace the workshop outcomes' benefits.

After reviewing the outcomes with them, ask,

> *Do you agree that if we accomplished these workshop outcomes, our team-building efforts would have been worth it?*

When the teammate says yes (even if their response is not very convincing!), affirm them. Tell them,

> *That's great news. It's important you believe that. I'm counting on you to do everything you can to make certain we have a good workshop. Can I count on you?*

With their consent, you've made a **pre-workshop agreement** and a pretty solid prevention plan. Of course, the next question to consider is, how will you intervene if this teammate becomes negative in the workshop despite your agreement?

Create an Intervention Plan

PCA, **Ground Rules**, and **Decision-Making Work Agreement** make up your prevention and intervention plan.

PCA is a facilitator tool that means Present, Clarify, and Agree. You should use this tool at the beginning of every team-building workshop, like this:

Present
- Kick off the meeting by presenting the workshop outcomes, ground rules, and Decision-Making Work Agreement.

Clarify
- Ask teammates if they have any clarifying questions. When you ask, be sure to pause; don't say anything for a short while.
- Typically, there are no questions because you have distributed the agenda ahead of time and have discussed it with any resistant teammate.
- Occasionally, someone may ask a simple question or add a new ground rule like, *It's okay to disagree, but it's not okay to be disrespectful or negative.*
- While you are waiting for questions, look into everyone's eyes. Do you see acceptance?

Agree
If you do see acceptance on people's faces, say,

Okay. It looks like everyone embraces the outcomes and agrees to abide by the ground rules and Decision-Making Agreement. Does everyone agree to do their part today?

Everyone says yes, and you're ready to move on.

Escalating Interventions

Even the best-planned workshops sometimes go sideways. It's essential to know how to intervene if things happen to go astray. When intervening, use an escalating intervention approach.

Always use the lowest level of intervention first.

Use lower-level interventions first. Only escalate to a mid-level intervention if low-level attempts are unsuccessful.

Lower-Level Interventions include:

- If a teammate becomes negative in the workshop, remind them of the outcomes and the agreed-upon ground rules or Decision-Making Agreement.

- Gently interrupt a tangent or escalating situation by "boomeranging" the non-stop talker's idea by asking another participant to comment on that idea.

- If there is a disruptive sidebar conversation that continues, slowly move towards the chatty teammates without saying a word. Often your presence alone will correct behavior.

Mid-Level Interventions include:

- Reflecting what you are seeing or hearing in the room without judgment. Saying, *I see /hear _____. What's going on?*

- If someone says something off-topic or not useful, find a portion of their statement you can accept and legitimize. Then either address their off-topic statement or ask for permission to defer the topic to the holding bin.

- If appropriate, use humor. But proceed with caution. Never make fun of anyone.

High-Level Interventions include:

- When there's a conflict or misunderstanding, ask the people in conflict to state the other's point of view to ensure mutual understanding.

- Take a break and talk with the agitated or disruptive person(s) offline. Taking time to understand their concerns can help create a way to get them back into collaboration.

- Confront the group or the specific people in conflict with the behavior you are seeing and hearing. Ask for ideas to resolve it.

Learning how to create and implement preventions and interventions is not hard but addressing conflict can initially be uncomfortable. However, it is part of your role as a facilitator. Like other team-building skills, you will get better and better at it the more you practice.

How to Design a
Right-Minded
TEAMWORK
Team-Building Workshop:
12-Step Process

Contract:
Designing
the Workshop

1 Start with the End in Mind ▼ Leader Defines Purpose

2 Leader Meets Facilitator ▼ Shares Purpose & Outcomes

Wants vs. Needs ▼ Facilitator Uncovers Root Causes 3

Facilitator Presents First Draft Plan to Leader 4

12 Leader & Facilitator Begin Designing the Second Workshop

11 Track & Report Progress for the Next 90 Days

Carry On: Continuing After the Workshop

10 Achieve Workshop Outcomes

Leader Announces Workshop & Prepares Teammates

Facilitator Conducts Right-Minded Teamwork Survey 5

Commence: Facilitating the Workshop

9 Leader & Facilitator Finalize Agenda & Workshop Plan

Facilitator Presents Second Draft Plan to Leader 8

Facilitator Interviews All Teammates 7

Facilitator Interviews All Teammates 6

Step 10 – Achieve Workshop Outcomes

This is it! It's finally time to see everything you've been working on come to life in your workshop.

In This Step, You Have Three Tasks

1. Prepare yourself.

2. Facilitate.

3. Properly close the workshop.

Prepare to Facilitate

The most effective facilitators prepare in advance and follow a formula for success.

Just like following RMT's 12-Step Process will consistently create powerful workshop experiences, taking the following steps will effectively prepare you for the workshop itself.

- Know your workshop outcomes and agenda. By now, you should almost have them memorized.

- Before the workshop, reaffirm preventions and interventions with the leader.

- Welcome everyone when they arrive and create a positive atmosphere.

- Use PCA: Present, Clarify, and gain Agreement on workshop outcomes during the kickoff.

- Plan to create a team decision-making agreement at the beginning of the workshop if one is not already in place.

- Briefly present the Right Choice Model at the beginning of the workshop, especially for problem-resolution meetings and ask everyone if they will conduct themselves in a Right-Minded accountable way.

- Be ready to present clear instructions for all exercises.

- Be prepared to interact with all teammates, especially difficult ones.

For more about successful facilitation and how to prepare, read the **14 Characteristics of a Successful Team Building Facilitator** *in the* **Resources** *section.*

Establish a Team Decision-Making Agreement

At the beginning of the workshop, I strongly recommend facilitating a short discussion that leads to a decision-making agreement for the workshop.

You might say, *"Our discussions today will result in creating Work Agreements. Ideally, we want to achieve consensus, which means that everyone will actively support these new Agreements.*

"But if for some reason, you simply can't come to a consensus as a team, your fallback method will be for the team leader to decide. Do you agree or disagree?"

Allow teammates to have a short discussion. Most of the time, they will all agree to this solution.

To solidify the decision-making agreement, say, *"To summarize, our decision-making agreement for this workshop is that you will first aim for consensus, and if that's not possible, your leader will be the fallback decider. Will everyone support this agreement?"*

Everyone says yes.

Facilitate the Creation of Team Work Agreements

Most Right-Minded Teamwork workshops result in the creation of one or more Work Agreements. No two Work Agreements are identical, but as you practice RMT with more and more clients, creating these Agreements will become second nature to you.

As you are learning and practicing, there are some specific steps you can choose to follow to create effective Work Agreements for any team.

*In the **Resources** section, you will find **Work Agreements: A Narrative Description of the 10 Facilitation Steps**.*

To learn how to facilitate work agreements, go to RightMindedTeamwork.com or your favorite book retailer and pick up your copy *How to Facilitate Team Work Agreements: A Practical, 10-Step Process for Building a Right-Minded Team That Works as One.*

Present the Right Choice Model

If you are facilitating a workshop that is similar to the true story I shared in Step 3, I encourage you to use the Right Choice Model. If you do, it will almost guarantee you will have a successful workshop.

To learn about the Choice Model, go to RightMindedTeamwork.com or your favorite book retailer and pick up **How to Apply the Right Choice Model:** *Create a Right-Minded Team That Works as One.* Look for the section titled: *"How to Present & Apply Right Choice in Your Team."*

But in the meantime, let me give you a quick introduction here.

Getting Prepared

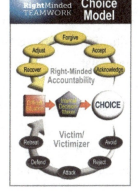

When you prepare to present the Right Choice concepts in a team-building workshop, your objective is to help teammates embrace Right-Minded Accountability while discussing they discuss their challenging issues. In this case, it will be a dissatisfied customer.

Your goal is to present the model in such a way that all teammates declare,

> *Of course, we need to approach our customer's disappointment in our service in a Right-Minded, accountable way. Let's get started.*

It's best to stick with a short presentation. Four to five minutes will suffice.

As soon as all teammates are in the right frame of mind, stop presenting, and move everyone into a team talk, a team discussion, where all teammates discuss and agree on how to solve their problem.

In this conversation, teammates use their right attitudes while discussing the issue. The discussion eventually leads to creating Work Agreements the teammates believe will resolve their issue.

After the workshop, teammates follow their Work Agreements. In time, because they have become more effective, your team has an even happier customer.

Difficult Situation: Your Customer's Demand

One of your team's primary customers just let your leader know they have become extremely disappointed in your team's service quality.

Your leader has decided the best way to address and resolve this situation is to conduct a problem-resolution session with all teammates.

About the Team

Your team is an Accounts Payable department consisting of 15 teammates, plus the leader.

Your team supports six large operating divisions. Every teammate is assigned to one or two specific operating divisions.

One of the operating division leaders recently informed your team leader that five out of the six key vendors they use for the last seven months were not paid on time.

This poor service has caused strained customer-vendor relationships for the operating division. The operations leader is very frustrated with your Accounts Payable department and wants their vendors paid on time.

They insist the A/P department fix the problem now.

Transiting From Your Customer's Demand
to Presenting the Right Choice Model

After the customer left your leader's office, where they insisted the A/P department fix their problem now, the leader called an emergency meeting with all 15 A/P teammates.

Everyone was asked to meet in the conference room in one hour.

To prepare, the leader printed the Right Choice Cards to give one to each teammate at the meeting.

An hour later, everyone was in the meeting room. The leader said,

> *We have a difficult situation. All of us need to band together to resolve it. Let me explain.*

The leader shared the details. The leader acknowledged the A/P department appeared to be paying the other five operating division's vendors on time. He went on to say,

> *Even though some of you are not directly involved with this situation, we are an interdependent team. We look out for and support one another.*

After we resolve this situation, we may likely need to use our new process improvements in all A/P functions. We will see, but we need to discuss and agree on how we will resolve the current problem now.

Before we start brainstorming potential solutions, I want to take just a few minutes to make sure we're all in the right frame of mind.

Recently, I saw this. It's called the Right Choice Model. [The leader distributes the Right Choice Cards to all.] *It's a simple way to describe right and wrong ways to address challenges like ours.*

The model teaches that we only have two choices regarding how we respond to challenges like this one. We either embrace and demonstrate Right-Minded attitudes and accountable behaviors, or we can lower ourselves into wrong-minded, victim behaviors.

Right Choice says, as you can see in the upper loop, we first need to acknowledge what has happened and accept our role in the situation. The third step is to forgive, or, if you prefer, stop blaming ourselves or others.

I firmly believe we can resolve this problem if we accept responsibility and forgive ourselves for what has happened. When we do that, we will create the right frame of mind to complete the last two steps of adjusting and recovering from this situation.

Our only other choice is to reject, attack, or defend, as you can see listed in the lower loop. If we go there, which is the wrong frame of mind, we will not resolve this problem. We are much better than that.

We are, by being here together right now, acknowledging this situation. We are accepting and owning our individual and team roles in this situation. And for goodness's sake, let's forgive ourselves and others so that we can be in the right frame of mind to find the best solutions.

Shall we all commit to demonstrating Right-Minded, upper loop, accountable behaviors in today's meeting so we can successfully recover and regain our customer's trust?

Everyone agreed. The leader continued,

Okay, great. What do we know about the situation, and what might be potential solutions?

Teammates brainstormed for two hours and created some new Work Agreements to streamline and speed up the payment process.

The next day, the leader and the two A/P teammates presented their work process improvement ideas to the operations leader.

All agreed that the new methods should work. The operations leader contacted the five vendors and explained the new process. The vendors were appreciative and cautiously optimistic. They agreed to wait and see if the new method worked.

Summary

In this story, you can easily see the basic formula for presenting Right Choice in your team:

- You present the Right Choice model while using the team's current difficult situation
- You facilitate a team talk that either leads to greater understanding or solutions to problems
- The understanding or solutions are captured in team Work Agreements
- Teammates commit to follow and live their team Work Agreements in hopes to recover and achieve customer satisfaction

In this situation, after learning about the difficult situation, the leader knew everyone on the team needed to band together to resolve it. The leader shared the dissatisfied customer's story with everyone, then used the Right Choice Model and Cards to create the right mindset for solving their problem. His presentation only lasted a few minutes.

Then he transitioned the conversation into team talk, a problem-resolution discussion, if you will, where they brainstormed solutions. The exchange resulted in Work Agreements that streamlined workflows and processes.

The team went back to the A/P's customer to share their solutions, and they looped in the vendor as well.

Following the team's implementation of their solutions, the vendor payments were never late again.

Properly Close the Workshop

Don't forget to allocate plenty of time to close the workshop correctly. A thorough closing takes at least 30 minutes.

To effectively close a workshop, you should:

- Review all Work Agreements to ensure clarity and the team's commitment to live them.

- Agree on how the team will track progress. Will they use a periodic team survey?

- Discuss and agree on the next 90 days' goals and actions.

- Agree that for the short term, the full team will review Work Agreements every week.

- For the remaining Punch List items, agree on when the team will address them (in another workshop?).

- List workshop positives as well as things to do differently in the next workshop.

- Ask teammates to share any gratitude or appreciation they have for others.

- Usually, the leader has the last word and adjourns the workshop. Often this will include thanking you, the facilitator, for your positive contributions to their team's success.

In the **Resources** section, read **Maria's Effective Workshop Close** to see how she praised her facilitator.

Your workshop has concluded, so you're off the hook, right?

Wrong!

. . . . .

Success is in the follow-up. In the next lesson, Step 11, we'll talk about how to keep the momentum going after your workshop is over.

How to Design a
Right-Minded
TEAMWORK
Team-Building Workshop:
12-Step Process

Contract:
Designing
the Workshop

1 Start with the End in Mind
Leader Defines Purpose

2 Leader Meets Facilitator
Shares Purpose & Outcomes

3 Wants vs. Needs
Facilitator Uncovers Root Causes

4 Facilitator Presents First Draft Plan to Leader

5 Leader Announces Workshop & Prepares Teammates

6 Facilitator Conducts Right-Minded Teamwork Survey

7 Facilitator Interviews All Teammates

8 Facilitator Presents Second Draft Plan to Leader

9 Leader & Facilitator Finalize Agenda & Workshop Plan

10 Achieve Workshop Outcomes

11 Track & Report Progress for the Next 90 Days

12 Leader & Facilitator Begin Designing the Second Workshop

Carry On: Continuing After the Workshop

Commence Facilitating the Workshop

Step 11 – Track & Report Progress for the Next 90 Days

As their facilitator, you'll want to support the team in tracking progress in the weeks and months following the workshop so they can see firsthand how effective their workshop was.

In This Step, You Have Two Tasks

1. Ensure the team designs and agrees upon a tracking method.

2. Determine how progress will be reported and to whom.

The Proof is in the Pudding

Rarely do teams resist the idea of tracking actual performance following the workshop. But don't be surprised if many of your teams don't follow through.

To ensure teams collect vital follow-up data, your job is to emphasize the importance of tracking. You'll need to continue sharing this message until the team actually experiences the benefits of tracking progress.

Once they see the benefits firsthand, your team will no longer need your constant encouragement and will gladly track for themselves.

Common & Effective Tracking Strategies

You will briefly discuss with your leader the topic of tracking team progress early in the design steps.

You'll want to discuss tracking again before the workshop outcomes and agenda are finalized.

In these conversations, your goal is to ensure the leader is in favor of tracking. You also want the leader to be prepared to propose tracking strategies if teammates don't suggest viable tracking solutions at the end of the workshop.

Here are several effective tracking strategies you can suggest:

Conduct the RMT 9 Right Choices Survey or 20-Question Team Perception Survey

- Survey within the first few weeks after the workshop, then every three months after that.

- The first two surveys will be valuable, but the third and subsequent ones will be even more valuable because they will reveal trends as they develop.

Take a look at a real example. Go to the **Resources** section, find **RMT Implementation Plan – 4 Actual Examples**, and find **Example #2 – Field Support Team**.

Team Performance Factor Assessment

If your team is using RMT's 5 Element process, then use the *Team Performance Factor Assessment* to track your team performance. For more information, see Step 6.

Identify 3-5 Current Process Measures to Track

- Teams may relate success to:
    - improved customer-supplier communications
    - reduced project-service mistakes
    - improved scheduling efficiencies

Create 1-2 Improvement Projects & Track Results

- For example, if team meetings could be more efficient, streamline the process and measure the improvement.

Take a look at a real example. Go to the **Resources** section, find **RMT Implementation Plan – 4 Actual Examples**, and find **Example #1 – Nuclear Power Generating Plant**.

Report Team Progress to Stakeholders

- When teammates make real progress, it motivates individuals to keep improving teamwork. When teams report their real improvement to their key stakeholders, it motivates teammates even more.

Take a look at a real example. Go to the **Resources** section, find **RMT Implementation Plan – 4 Actual Examples**, and find **Example #2 – Field Support Team**.

Fine-Tune Work Agreements

- Conduct one-to-two-minute Work Agreement "reminder moments" at the beginning of team meetings to remind everyone of the Agreement essentials.

- Conduct a 30-minute fine-tuning discussion within two weeks of the workshop and every six weeks after that.

    o Over time, as teammates begin to live the Agreements more habitually, the team can gradually abandon their Agreement "reminder moments" and reviews.

    o But in the first few weeks and months, it's vitally important that teams receive regular reminders of their Agreements to encourage the necessary behavioral change.

A Note About Fine-Tuning Work Agreements

Creating Work Agreements is only 50% of the improvement effort.

The other 50% is *living* those Work Agreements.

Whether teammates willingly engage and fine-tune their Agreements in the first few weeks says a lot about whether they're actually going to live them.

So, remind your team:

To make your Agreement means nothing.
To live by your Agreement means everything.

Here are a few lessons I learned about fine-tuning Work Agreements:

- It is normal for teams to experience buoyed spirits, extra enthusiasm, newfound commitment to goals, or a burst of higher performance after the initial workshop.

  o This "halo effect" will not last for more than two to three weeks, which is why teams must spend time reviewing, fine-tuning, and re-committing to their Work Agreements.

- It is impossible and impractical to think that everyone will live the Agreements perfectly.

  o Therefore, living them perfectly is not the only goal. Being able to *recover* when a teammate breaks the Agreement is an equally important part of their goal.

- Expect that some teammates will remain skeptical of their Work Agreements even after they have participated in creating them.

  o Encourage them by saying, *"If you keep the Agreements and hold others accountable in a safe and supportive way, the Agreements will work. I've seen it happen on many other teams that had challenges just like yours."*

IMPORTANT: As you catch teammates living the spirit and letter of their Agreement, praise them.

Now, over the next 90 days, teammates will do their best to improve their teamwork and track their progress.

In the **Resources** *section, you will find a* **Report of Improvement** *template your team can use.*

Also, in **Resources**, you'll find **Work Agreements Bring People Together as One**, a real-world example of how one team used the 20-Question Team Perception Survey as a way to track actual performance.

· · · · ·

Around day 70, it's time for our final lesson, Step 12, where you'll reach back out to the team leader to connect and discuss the next steps.

How to Design a
Right-Minded
TEAMWORK
Team-Building Workshop:
12-Step Process

Contract:
Designing
the Workshop

1 Start with the
End in Mind
▼
Leader
Defines
Purpose

Leader Meets
Facilitator
▼
Shares
Purpose
&
Outcomes
2

Wants vs. Needs
▼
Facilitator
Uncovers
Root Causes
3

Facilitator Presents
First Draft
Plan to Leader
4

Leader Announces
Workshop &
Prepares
Teammates
5

Facilitator
Conducts
Right-Minded
Teamwork
Survey

Facilitator
Interviews
All
Teammates
6

7

Facilitator
Presents
Second Draft
Plan
to Leader
8

9 Leader &
Facilitator
Finalize Agenda
&
Workshop
Plan

Commence:
Facilitating
the
Workshop

10 Achieve
Workshop
Outcomes

Carry On:
Continuing
After the
Workshop

11 Track & Report
Progress for
the Next 90 Days

12
Leader &
Facilitator
Begin Designing
the
Second
Workshop

Step 12 – Design the Second Workshop

With one successful workshop complete, it's time for the team to continue their forward progress.

You know your team has more items on their Punch List, so another workshop is in order.

In This Step, You Have Two Tasks

1. Schedule a workshop design meeting with the team leader.

2. You transfer design and facilitation responsibilities to the team leader or re-contract to design and facilitate the second workshop.

Transfer Responsibilities or Re-Contract

When you ended the workshop two months ago, you and the leader agreed you would call to schedule a follow-up meeting.

- When that day comes (around day 60-70 after the workshop), you and the leader will discuss the following:

- What has the team achieved?

- What does the team still need to achieve? (the remainder of their Punch List)

- When do you want to schedule the second workshop?

- Would you like for me to help you design and facilitate that workshop?

  o If yes, ask the team leader to assign two teammates to work with you to eventually take responsibility for future team building.

IMPORTANT

Successful RMT facilitators find joy in transferring their design and facilitation skills to their teams.

So be glad if the team is ready to learn how to support their own growth and facilitation! The rewards for teaching and transferring these skills are great.

It is likely the leader will want your support in planning the next workshop. To get the ball rolling in this initial conversation, you can say,

> *During the next workshop, let's be certain to celebrate lessons learned and include time to fine-tune our Work Agreements.*
>
> *Let's also administer the teammate survey again. I'll interview all the teammates, just like before, and create a second version of our Punch List.*
>
> *And, since it worked so well last time, let's also follow the same 12-Step Right-Minded Teamwork workshop process.*

If you followed all the steps the first time and conducted a practical Right-Minded Teamwork workshop that led to tangible team results, your leader will gladly agree.

Which means...

You've officially completed the last step of the 12-Step Right-Minded Teamwork Teambuilding Workshop. Hooray!

However, it doesn't stop here. It's time to start over at Step 1 as you begin the process of designing the second workshop!

The End.
Your New Beginning.

When all 5 Elements of Right-Minded Teamwork's core framework are fully released into your client team's operating system, including RMT's 12-Steps design process, you have, as their team-building facilitator, helped them to establish the proper condition for successfully achieving Right-Minded Teamwork

Ask Your Team to Imagine...

You are now thinking and behaving in a Right-Minded way. You are self-aware and focused on achieving your **team's business** and **psychological goals**. You consistently strive for **100% customer satisfaction**, and you always aim to **do no harm** while **working as one**.

To guide your steps, you have purposeful team **Work Agreements** describing your team's thought system. You get work done by leveraging your **Team Operating System**, identifying the critical-few, focusing on solutions, and making true improvements.

As Right-Minded Teammates, you **willfully follow Reason**, behaving mindfully and positively navigating difficult team situations. You have risen far above Ego's battleground to joyfully engage with one another in your work classroom, learning and growing every day. Happily, you find yourselves living more and more often in the **Unified Circle of Right-Minded Teamwork Thinking.**

Your New Beginning as a Right-Minded Teamwork Facilitator

Now that you understand each of RMT's 5 Elements and how they will benefit your client team, you are ready to implement RMT. Remember, even though there is no right way to implement RMT, the three-workshop Implementation Plan presented earlier in these pages will always work.

So, conduct the first workshop. Help teammates live their new team Work Agreements for a month or two and then conduct the second workshop. Trust the process. Keep them moving forward.

When they finish the third teammate development workshop, they will begin following their customized 90-Day team operating plan. Every quarter, they will measure their progress and success. Each time, they will reinforce the value of RMT in their team.

Don't Forget!

As you begin your journey as a Right-Minded Teamwork facilitator, don't forget: good facilitation does not just happen on its own. You must practice and learn.

To bring your client teams together, you need guidance from proven, real-world methods, such as Right-Minded Teamwork. Moreover, you need to encourage your teammates to sincerely want to receive and follow this guidance, or the powerful teachings will be meaningless. Good teamwork must be a collaborative venture of commitment and growth.

Say to them,

> *If you want better teamwork, Right-Minded Teamwork can show you how to get there and what to do, but only with your help. Together with your teammates, you must believe that you have what it takes. With that conviction and Reason's guidance, you will collectively create and sustain Right-Minded Teamwork.*
>
> *Now, go and create Right-Minded Teamwork for yourself and your team, and know that **you are making the world better for everyone, everywhere, forever.***

The End

Thanks for reading our Right-Minded Teamwork book. If you enjoyed it, won't you please take a moment to leave a review at your favorite retailer or RightMindedTeamwork.com?

Also, in a few pages, you will find something beneficial: a ***Glossary of Right-Minded Teamwork Terms and Resources.***

And finally, on behalf of Reason and all the Right-Minded Teammate Decision-Makers and facilitators, we extend our best wishes to you and your teammates as they create another ***Right-Minded Team that Works Together as One***.

DECISION MAKER

REASON

About the Author

The idea of "developing people and teams that work" began as a company statement for organizational consulting firm Lord & Hogan LLC, founded in 1990. Leveraging his personable but results-oriented consulting style, founder **Dan Hogan** devoted his career to transforming dysfunctional work relationships into positive, supportive bonds.

But over the course of his 40-year career, something shifted.

Through his work as an organizational development coach, performance consultant, and Certified Master Facilitator, the mission of Lord & Hogan also became Dan's own.

Better Work Relationships = Stronger, More Productive Teams

As a consultant and facilitator, Dan advocated for the individuals and managed teams he served. He emphasized the equal importance of strong team member relationships and solid business systems and processes to overall business success. His efforts spoke for themselves as his clients began to notice results.

With Dan's guidance, teams were more productive almost overnight. There were fewer day-to-day interpersonal issues. Project management efforts were finally back on track. Teams were achieving their goals.

After being stuck for so long, these teams were moving forward... smoothly. As one client said, "Dan has the unique ability to hear the confusion and bring clarity. He has helped me, our team, and our organization to move to the next level."

The Right-Minded Teamwork Model: A Legacy

Not only did Dan's efforts deliver consistent, powerful results (gaining him many long-term clients over the years) at a higher level, his work also positively impacted the practice of behavioral change management.

Over the course of his career, Dan refined his ideas along with the help of his clients and the teams he served. Eventually, he created his own proprietary tools, processes, and strategies. Of all his models and creations, Dan's most significant accomplishment has been the development of his Right-Minded Teamwork model, which perfectly assembles all his tools and processes into a single, streamlined approach.

At its core, Right-Minded Teamwork (RMT) is a continuous improvement loop for small and large groups; it has been proven to work with teams of all sizes. No matter what team challenges or interpersonal issues are happening, RMT has the power to correct them.

By first bringing the team together under a unified set of goals, then providing tools for teams to explore, understand, and work through their underlying concerns, Right-Minded Teamwork provides teams with the opportunity to address unproductive behaviors in a safe, non-condemning way. Focusing on acceptance, forgiveness, and self-adjustment among teammates, Right-Minded Teamwork directly addresses and resolves the root cause of even the most difficult teamwork situations.

After directly serving over 500 teams in seven countries and creating lasting tools and resources that will go on to support countless additional teams, leaders, and facilitators on every continent, Dan Hogan has left a legacy to be proud of. No longer an active facilitator, Dan has transformed his ideas and contributions into powerful, effective, team-building tools available online, providing team facilitators and team leaders around the globe access to Right-Minded Teamwork.

Books by Dan Hogan

Reason, Ego & the Right-Minded Teamwork Myth: The Philosophy and Process for Creating a Right-Minded Team That Works Together as One

This book explores two foundational concepts: the Right-Minded Teamwork Myth, a short tale that presents RMT's underlying teamwork philosophy, and the Right-Minded Teamwork team-building process, a step-by-step approach to implementing RMT in any team.

Right-Minded Teamwork in Any Team: The Ultimate Team-Building Method to Create a Team That Works as One

Right-Minded Teamwork is built on a framework of 5 Elements, explored in this book. These two goals and three methods are implemented into your team through three team-building workshops conducted over a six-to-12-month period. Once your team completes their third workshop, you move into a 90-day, continuous improvement operating plan that allows your team to achieve their goals, do no harm and work together as one.

How to Facilitate Team Work Agreements*: A Practical, 10-Step Process for Building a Right-Minded Team That Works as One*

Team Work Agreements are collective pledges made by your team to transform non-productive or dysfunctional actions into positive and constructive work behavior. Though this book is written primarily for team facilitators, team leaders and teammates may also follow these steps to create powerful, effective Work Agreements to solve and prevent interpersonal and process problems.

How to Apply the Right Choice Model*: Create a Right-Minded Team That Works as One*

The concept of Right Choice states every person has free will. Free will means you are 100% responsible for how you respond to every situation, circumstance, and event. When difficult team problems occur, you either act as an ally or an adversary. When you choose to be an ally, you demonstrate positive, accountable behavior. When you are an adversary, you behave as either a victim or a victimizer. This book and model will guide you through creating a team of productive, supportive, Right-Minded teammate allies.

*7 **Mindfulness Training Lessons***: *Improve Teammates' Ability to Work as One with Right-Minded Thinking*

If you want your team working together as one, you want them thinking as one, too. These 7 Mindfulness Training Lessons will help you achieve a positive team mindset by guiding teammates to raise their awareness of thoughts, choices, and behaviors. Teammates may also use these lessons to create the team's Right-Minded thought system. The 7 Lessons can be summed up in one sentence, emphasizing three words: Right-Minded Teammates **accept**, **forgive**, and **adjust** their thinking and work behavior. When teammates follow these lessons, they **do no harm** while **working together as one.**

Right-Minded Teamwork: *9 Right Choices for Building a Team That Works as One*

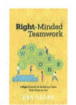

This quick read is an excellent Right-Minded Teamwork primer and a terrific way to introduce RMT to teammates. These nine teamwork choices are universal, self-evident, and self-validating. You want them in your team. In this book, each of the 9 Right Choices is defined, and exercises are provided for applying each choice.

Design a Right-Minded, Team-Building Workshop*:
12 Steps to Create a Team That Works as One*

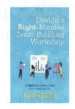

This book includes complete instruction on how to design
a practical, real-world, team-building workshop that
teammates actually want to attend. Unlike many team activities
labeled "team building" that are really more "team bonding," true
team-building workshops are intentionally designed to solve a team's
real-world problems. Written primarily for team facilitators, team
leaders and teammates may also follow these 12 steps to design an
effective, transformative team workshop.

Achieve Your Organization's Strategic Plan*: Create a
Right-Minded Team Management System to Ensure All
Teams Work as One*

When a single team within an organization works together
as one, they are effective and productive. When an enterprise works
with the same level of synergy, it is exponentially more powerful. A
Team Management System, like the Right-Minded Teamwork TMS
model taught in this book, lays the groundwork for your organization
to get every team on the same page. By following RMT's four-part
rollout plan, create and deploy your own Team Management System,
align teammate attitudes and work behavior with company values, and
bring your entire organization together to work as one and achieve
your strategic plan.

Find Dan Hogan & Right-Minded Teamwork Online

Visit my website: https://rightmindedteamwork.com

Subscribe to my blog: Teamwork News:
https://rightmindedteamwork.com/blog

Friend me on LinkedIn: https://www.linkedin.com/in/danalanhogan/

Follow me on Facebook:
https://www.facebook.com/RightMindedTeamwork

Favorite my Smashwords Author Page:
https://www.smashwords.com/profile/view/rightmindedteamwork

Read my Smashwords Interview:
https://www.smashwords.com/interview/rightmindedteamwork

Follow me on Amazon Author Page: https://amzn.to/3noStKA

Glossary of
Right-Minded Teamwork
Terms & Resources

100% Customer Satisfaction

Creating 100% customer satisfaction is a primary goal of Right-Minded Teamwork. Your team is responsible for providing quality products and services to customers; for your team and enterprise to succeed, your customers deserve to be 100% satisfied.

With a strong customer satisfaction plan, as described in *Right-Minded Teamwork in Any Team*, your teammates will strive to achieve customer satisfaction while consistently achieving other business goals.

7 Mindfulness Training Lessons

Achieving Right-Minded Teamwork involves adopting an attitude of mindfulness. The *7 Mindfulness Training Lessons* teach you to think in a Right-Minded way, ensuring you **do no harm** as you **work as one** with your teammates.

These powerful lessons are summed up in one sentence, with emphasis on three words:

Right-Minded Teammates **accept**, **forgive**, *and* **adjust** *their thinking and work behavior.*

In every circumstance, especially during difficult team situations, Right-Minded Teammates practice mindfulness to move them from defensiveness and blame into a Right-Minded, allied way of thinking and behaving.

Inspired by *A Course in Miracles* and our Right Choice Model, the *7 Mindfulness Training Lessons* is a teaching tool designed to help those willing to apply them to ensure they return to the Unified Circle of Right-Minded Thinking.

Go to RightMindedTeamwork.com or visit your favorite book retailer to pick up your copy of *7 **Mindfulness Training Lessons**: Improve Teammates' Ability to Work as One with Right-Minded Thinking.*

10 Characteristics of Right-Minded Teammates

Right-Minded Teammates have many different surface traits and personalities. They are not all alike. They have numerous backgrounds, vastly different experiences, and a wide range of skills.

Nevertheless, it is understood that the Right-Minded Teammate, in their own particular behavioral style, happily live these characteristics because they align the teammate's authentic *self* with their team's version of the RMT motto: *do no harm*, *work as one*, and *none of us is as smart as all of us.*

You will find a complete description of these characteristics in RMT's book: ***Right-Minded Teamwork in Any Team:*** *The Ultimate Team Building Method to Create a Team That Works as One.*

1. Trust	2. Honesty	3. Tolerance
4. Gentleness	5. Joy	6. Defenselessness
7. Generosity	8. Patience	9. Open-Mindedness
	10. Faithfulness	

12 Steps Workshop Design Process

Design a Right-Minded, Team-Building Workshop: *12 Steps to Create a Team That Works as One.* This book will teach you how to design a practical, real-world team-building workshop.

The 12 steps are grouped into three phases: Contract, Commence, and Carry on. Written primarily for team facilitators, team leaders, and teammates can easily follow the steps to design a successful team-building workshop. Because this method engages teammates in designing the agenda, it virtually guarantees that teammates *cannot wait* to attend the workshop. They *know* that they will get real work done in a safe, "no harm" environment when they meet.

A Course in Miracles

Oneness. Forgiveness is the key to happiness, inner peace, undifferentiated unity, and ultimately – *oneness*. "A Course In Miracles (ACIM) is a unique spiritual self-study program designed to awaken us to the truth of our *oneness* with God and Love," as posted on ACIM.org and ACIM.org/ACIM/en. See the Foundation for A Course in Miracles at FACIM.org, where Ken Wapnick, the founder, created this beautiful definition.

A Course in Miracles is a psychological approach to spirituality where forgiveness is the central theme, and inner peace is the result.

ACIM and other moral and spiritual philosophies that advocate and help people everywhere **work together as One** has inspired Right-Minded Teamwork. We used Ken's definition as a guide to create the Right-Minded Teamwork definition.

Right-Minded Teamwork is a business-oriented, psychological approach to team building where acceptance, forgiveness, and adjustments are teammate characteristics, and 100% customer satisfaction is the team's result.

All Right-Minded Teamwork methods, processes, and tools seamlessly work together to help you create and sustain a *Team That Works Together as **One**.*

Accept, Forgive, Adjust

These three terms are at the core of Right-Minded Teammate Attitudes & Behaviors. These verbs are also central to the *7 Mindfulness Training Lessons*, which are summed up in the sentence, *Right-Minded Teammates **accept**, **forgive**, and **adjust** their thinking and work behavior.*

Furthermore, these three concepts are included in the definition of Right-Minded Teamwork:

*Right-Minded Teamwork is a business-oriented, psychological approach to team building where **acceptance**, **forgiveness**, and **adjustment** are teammate characteristics, and 100% customer satisfaction is the team's result.*

Lastly, these terms are also incorporated as three of the five steps in the *Right Choice Model*, which describes accountable and responsible Right-Minded Teamwork behavior.

Ally or Adversary Teammate

Right-Minded Teamwork asserts that as teammates, you either work together as allies, or you pull apart, viewing each other as adversaries.

Allies work towards achieving team goals. Adversaries work towards individual elevation, which separates and divides the team.

To determine whether you are in an ally or adversary mindset, ask yourself, *Do I want to be right, or do I want our team to be successful?* Allies want to be part of a successful team. Adversaries want to be right, no matter the cost.

As an adversary, Ego persuades you to compete with your teammates. As an ally, Reason says the opposite. Reason gently reminds you that separateness prevents true success. There cannot be oneness or collaboration where there is competition.

As the Decision-Maker, you choose to follow either Reason or Ego. You either collaborate or compete. You are an ally or adversary. There is no middle ground.

If you choose to follow Reason and become an ally, you embrace and live your team's Work Agreements. If you decide to follow Ego, you become an adversary, creating a battleground inside yourself and your team.

To transform competitive adversaries into collaborative allies, start by following the *Right Choice Model*, creating team *Work Agreements*, and applying the *7 Mindfulness Training Lessons*.

Avoidance Behavior

Even though the term "avoidance behavior" is not often mentioned in the Right-Minded Teamwork model or books, avoidance behavior is easy to detect in teammates and RMT processes. If you notice it occurring, from an RMT perspective, you can consider it wrong-minded, adversarial behavior.

Identifying avoidance behaviors and attitudes and understanding the harm they cause is the first step in moving from a wrong-minded place into Right-Mindedness. The *7 Mindfulness Training Lessons* and the *Right Choice Model* are excellent tools for teaching yourself and your team how to act and behave in a Right-Minded, accountable way.

For example, if you look carefully at the *Right Choice Model's* lower loop, you will notice that the victim or victimizer first avoids the situation when a difficult situation occurs.

When Right-Minded Teammates ask themselves the *Right Choice Model* question, *How did I **create**, **promote**, or **allow** this difficult situation to happen?* they often realize they have unconsciously demonstrated avoidance behavior. Then, noticing their mistake, they simply choose to **accept**, **forgive**, and **adjust** their approach and return to living in accordance with their team *Work Agreements*.

Battleground:
Where People Are Punished for Mistakes

The battleground represents wrong-minded thinking. It is a mental attitude or thought system that defends and encourages adversarial behaviors such as blame and attack.

Think of the battleground as a psychological symbol for those moments when you realize you are listening to Ego, not Reason (like when you notice avoidance behavior). You recognize that you are having an Ego attack for whatever reason and have made a wrong-minded choice. When you are in the battleground, you "punish" others for their mistakes, either by victimizing others or becoming a victim yourself.

On the other hand, when you are in your right mind, you see your team as a lovely and safe classroom, the opposite of the battleground. You do not punish others. You choose, instead, to rise above the conflict.

The purpose of recognizing the battlegrounds in your mind is to own the pain that you are causing yourself which helps you recognize that you consciously want to leave it, overlook it, rise above it, and to transport your mind into the classroom where you return to the forgiving Unified Circle of Right-Minded Thinking with your teammates.

Right-Minded Teammates working in safe and supportive classrooms do not fight, blame, or punish. Instead, they choose oneness over separateness. They are committed to the team's success and achieving team goals.

To overcome a battleground in yourself or your team, go to RightMindedTeamwork.com, or visit your favorite book retailer to pick up your copy of *How to Apply the Right Choice Model: Create a Right-Minded Team That Works as One*. Inside, you will find a list of battleground attitudes and behaviors as well as the costs and benefits of classroom versus battleground thinking and behaving.

Certified Master Facilitator (CMF)

The Certified Master Facilitator (CMF) credential is a mark of excellence for facilitators. It is the highest available certification for facilitators. To learn more or to find a certified facilitator worldwide, visit the International Institute for Facilitation at INIFAC.org.

Classroom:
Where People Learn from Mistakes

Like the battleground, the classroom is a symbol. But unlike the battlefield, where people punish or are punished, the classroom is where you learn and find inspiration.

At some point in your past, you have experienced the joy and wonder of learning. Right-Minded Teamwork invites you to view your team as a safe place to experience this wonder and joy as you learn new teamwork skills and collaborate to achieve team goals.

When you are experiencing fear in any form or realize you are having an Ego attack, you are in the battleground. To return to the classroom, say to yourself, *There is nothing to fear. In my mind, I choose to rise above this silly battleground and head to my Right-Minded classroom. There, we are committed to do no harm and work as one. There, we will find solutions.*

By recognizing the fear behind your Ego attack and reminding yourself to return to the classroom, you experience a **moment of Reason**. You also strengthen your Right-Minded thought system and restore yourself to Right-Minded Thinking.

In the RMT book *How to Apply the Right Choice Model: Create a Right-Minded Team That Works as One,* you will find a list of 30 Right-Minded and wrong-minded attitudes and behaviors, plus the associated costs and benefits to your team.

Communication Work Agreement

What you think – *your thought system* – drives your communication in one of two ways. You either communicate as a collaborative ally or as a competitive, dysfunctional, and emotionally immature adversary.

Teams that work as one and achieve their goals regularly seek out opportunities to improve communication. They take positive action by creating and living a Communication Work Agreement that describes their team's agreed-upon communication style.

Right-Minded communication is a core concept in the book *Right-Minded Teamwork: 9 Right Choices for Building a Team That Works as One*, available at RightMindedTeamwork.com or your favorite book retailer.

To create your team's Communication Work Agreement, follow the suggestions in the book *How to Facilitate Teamwork Agreements: A Practical, 10-Step Process for Building a Right-Minded Team That Works as One*.

In there, you will find two real examples of which one is a team Communication Work Agreement.

Create, Promote, Allow

These three concepts form the foundation of the *Right Choice Model's* essential question:

*How have I **created**, **promoted**, or **allowed** this situation to occur?*

Asking and honestly answering this question ensures teammates are "owning their part" in a difficult situation.

These three concepts are also integrated into *7 **Mindful Training Lessons**: Improve Teammate's Ability to Work as One with Right-Minded Thinking.*

High-performing Right-Minded Teammates always ask themselves this question because it leads them to solutions. It is a clear demonstration of the RMT motto, "**Do no harm. Work as one.**"

Critical Few:
Complete Important Tasks First

When a team is stuck in the "full-plate syndrome," identifying and completing the critical few - those tasks that have the largest and most direct impact on the team's success - is key to moving forward.

At the root of the full-plate syndrome is the **team's collective fear**, driven by Ego, which declares you will get in trouble if you do not do it all… even though the truth is you can never do it all.

People who listen to Ego believe they do not have a choice. Rather than realistically prioritizing their workload, they punish themselves for failing to meet the unreasonable goal of completing everything. They drain their energy, lose their focus, and make mistakes. They become powerless, cynical, and burned out.

But Reason reminds us that we always have this choice:

We can either win by doing the critical few tasks, or we can lose by attempting to do everything.

Spend more time doing the right things right and let go of low-value tasks. Holding on to lower-value tasks is **not security**. It is **incarceration**.

The "critical few" concept is discussed in the book ***Right-Minded Teamwork***: *9 Right Choices for Building a Team That Works as One*.

See **Recognition: Make It Easy to Keep Going** for a related concept.

Decision-Maker: The Real You

Ken Wapnick, Ph.D., created the term "Decision-Maker" to define the "real you" in *A Course in Miracles*. For more on his work, visit FACIM.org.

Within Right-Minded Teamwork, the *Right Choice Model* uses the term "Decision-Maker" to describe the part of you that chooses to listen to and follow either the wrong-minded ways of Ego or the Right-Minded ways of Reason.

Your Decision-Maker is 100% responsible for who you choose to follow, what you choose to think, and how you choose to behave.

Right-Mindedness is achieved when you listen to and follow Reason. Listening means calming your Ego mind, trusting your intuition, and allowing space for a **moment of Reason** to arise.

When Right-Mindedness becomes an integral part of a team, the team consistently works together as one, doing no harm, within the forgiving Unified Circle of Right-Minded Thinking. When teammates do that, they are demonstrating and extending Right-Minded Teamwork to everyone.

To learn more about Reason, Ego, and the Decision-Maker, visit RightMindedTeamwork.com or your favorite book retailer and pick up the book *Reason, Ego, & the Right-Minded Teamwork Myth: The Philosophy & Process for Creating a Right-Minded Team That Works Together as One*. The ebook is free. It's also available in paperback.

Decision-Maker: Trust Your Intuition

If thinking about Reason and Ego are new to you, it can be helpful to think of Reason as your positive intuition and Ego as your negative, arrogant, and sometimes vindictive intuition.

At different times throughout our lives, we all have listened to and followed each of these teachers.

Stop and remember when you had a hunch or a feeling as to what you should do or say in a particular situation. Did you ignore your intuition? Let's say you did not follow your instinct, and it turned out to be a mistake. What did you say to yourself and others?

> *I wish I had trusted my intuition!*

As this memory illustrates, **you already know how to listen and be mindful** of your intuition. It is your natural, pre-separation state of mind [See **Oneness vs. Separateness**].

You just need to do it regularly.

Decision-Making Work Agreement

Every team needs a Decision-Making Work Agreement that clearly defines how decisions are made and who makes them. Creating a general agreement and putting it into your team's Operating System's Business Plan as a team Work Agreement makes good business sense.

If you do not currently have a Decision-Making team agreement or you have not updated it recently, I highly recommend you do that as soon as it is practical.

Incidentally, Decision-Making is #18 in the *Team Performance Factor Assessment* that you will use every 90 days to keep your team focused and on track. See **Team Operating System**.

In the book, ***How to Facilitate Team Work Agreements****: A Practical, 10-Step Process for Building a Right-Minded Team That Works as One,* you will find two real agreement examples. The first one is a behavioral team Communication Work Agreement, and the other is a Decision-Making Work Agreement. Check it out and use it as a model for your team's Decision-Making Work Agreement.

Desire & Willingness:
Preconditions for Accountability

Even though the terms "desire" and "willingness" are not often mentioned in Right-Minded Teamwork materials (except within the *Right Choice Model*), Right-Mindedness and accountability are virtually synonymous.

The concepts of desire and willingness permeate all RMT methods and processes simply because it is impossible to think in a Right-Minded way, behave with Right-Minded Accountability, and achieve Right-Minded Teamwork without a heartfelt desire and genuine willingness to do so.

The *Right Choice Model* found in the book ***How to Apply the Right Choice Model****: Create a Right-Minded Team That Works as One* teaches, *Right-Minded Accountability is the desire and willingness to change my mind and behavior in order to effectively respond to difficult team situations.*

If you share the Right Choice Model with your team and distribute the Right Choice cards to teammates, you will see the definition of "desire and willingness" on the cards.

Ego & Ego Attack

Ego is the negative, wrong-minded teacher who continually tells you how difficult the world is and how you must constantly fight to survive.

EGO

Reason is the opposite of Ego. Reason teaches you to *do unto others as you would have them do unto you.*

Ego believes everyone is out to get you and directs you to *do unto others before they do unto you.* Ego is also the creator of the tiny, mad idea of separation presented in the *Right-Minded Teamwork Myth.*

An Ego attack is a flash of negative, out-of-control emotion. It happens when you believe the awful feeling you are experiencing has been caused by something someone else said or did to you. Without thinking, you become behaviorally triggered; your body language, tone of voice, and the words you say become mean-spirited. An Ego attack is the opposite of a **moment of Reason**.

As soon as you realize you are experiencing an Ego attack, you must train your mind to say, *I am angry. I have lost control. I'm not upset for the reason I think. I am out of my right mind. I need a moment of Reason to gain control of my attitude. I must return to the classroom so I can find a Right-Minded way of replying that allows us to do no harm and work as one.*

Interlocking Accountability

Interlocking accountability is a crucial RMT concept that is primarily used in *How to Facilitate Team Work Agreements: a Practical, 10-Step Process for Building a Right-Minded Team That Works as One.*

When your team creates Work Agreements, it is highly recommended that one of your agreements includes an interlocking accountability statement so that teammates agree, ahead of time, how to compassionately confront a teammate who continues to break your Work Agreements.

Interlocking Accountability means many things, including:

- Giving positive reinforcement when someone continues to do a great job of living the Work Agreements.
- Confronting someone in a supportive and safe but firm way if they continue to break the spirit or letter of the team's Work Agreement.
- Being accountable to each other for achieving or accomplishing the desired outcome of the Work Agreements.
- Recovering and learning from mistakes rather than denying or punishing those who make mistakes. This strengthens team spirit and trust.
- Creating and sustaining teammate trust because teammates who believe everyone will live their part of the Work Agreement will create Right-Minded Teamwork.

Moment of Reason

When you are facing a challenge such as an Ego attack, and you experience a positive and perhaps surprising moment of revelation, clarity, or sanity, you have achieved a moment of Reason.

These moments occur when you genuinely try to move from the battleground into the classroom. When Reason's teaching breaks through, you move from wrong mindedness into Right-Mindedness.

Moments of Reason are magnificent. They are a cornerstone of your Right-Minded thought system. When they happen, you feel confident and at peace. You know what you should do, what to say, and to whom.

In moments of Reason, you know beyond a shadow of a doubt that you want and need your teammates. You easily return to the Unified Circle of Right-Minded Thinking, where teammates forgive one another, do no harm, and work as one.

Onboarding New Teammates

When a new leader or teammate joins your team, it is vitally important to properly onboard them within their first week on the job. In a single short meeting where everyone attends, the onboarding is easily and effectively accomplished.

Present all your RMT goals and Work Agreements along with why they were created. They ask you clarifying questions. Afterward, you ask them to accept the team's goals and actively live the team's Work Agreements.

Oneness vs. Separateness

Oneness is a psychological state of mind. It can be described in many ways using phrases such as *None of us is as smart as all of us,* or *do no harm,* and *work as one.*

Separateness is the opposite of oneness. To become a Right-Minded teammate, you must train your mind to choose attitudes and behaviors that create and extend oneness, not project separateness.

For a list of 30 examples of oneness, see the Right-Minded Teamwork Attitudes & Behaviors list found in numerous RMT books.

The concepts and story behind oneness and separateness are introduced in RMT's book, ***Reason, Ego & the Right-Minded Teamwork Myth:*** *The Philosophy and Process for Creating a Right-Minded Team That Works Together as One.* You can pick up your ebook copy for free at RightMindedTeamwork.com or your favorite book retailer. It is also available in paperback.

In this book, you will learn about Ego's "tiny, mad idea" of wanting more "stuff" and how Ego's choices led us all into a world of separation. That tiny, mad moment was, literally, the **birth of separation**. But, as the Myth reveals, Reason is always ready to lead us back into oneness - our pre-separation state – joyfully described as the Unified Circle of Right-Minded Thinking where we can do no harm and work as one.

Preventions & Interventions

In RMT's ***Design a Right-Minded, Team-Building Workshop****: 12 Steps to Create a Team That Works as One*, the team-building facilitator and team leader meet early on to proactively identify potential issues that could keep teammates from achieving the workshop's desired outcomes.

This discussion leads to creating *preventions* that the team leader or facilitator takes to help prevent those issues from happening. The facilitator and team leader also agree on how to intervene in case the preventions don't work. Much of the time, however, preventions do their job and make *interventions* during team-building workshops unnecessary.

To learn more about effective preventions and interventions, go to RightMindedTeamwork.com or your favorite book retailer, and pick up your copy of these two books:

How to Facilitate Team Work Agreements*: A Practical, 10-Step Process for Building a Right-Minded Team That Works as One*

Design a Right-Minded, Team-Building Workshop*: 12 Steps to Create a Team That Works as One*

Psychological Goals

A team's psychological goals describe how teammates intentionally choose to think and behave as they work together to achieve their team's business goals.

Psychological goals, such as achieving mutual trust and respect among teammates, may be viewed as a team's collective school of thought, values, or thought system.

These consciously chosen goals, captured in team Work Agreements, clarify the team's principles or standards of behavior.

Here is a specific example of a psychological goal you will find in several RMT materials:

> *When difficult team situations happen, we accept, forgive, and adjust our attitudes and behavior. We always find solutions because we believe that none of us is as smart as all of us.*

Reason

Reason is a mythological character and symbolic guide who shows you how to think and behave in a Right-Minded way. As your Right-Minded teacher, Reason helps you differentiate and choose between Right-Minded and wrong-minded attitudes and behaviors.

REASON

Reason is the opposite of Ego. Whereas Ego believes everyone is out to get you and instructs you to *do unto others before they do unto you,* Reason teaches you to *do unto others as you would have them do unto you.*

Ego encourages and projects separateness.
Reason cultivates and extends oneness.

Reason is that part of your mind that always speaks for the Right Choice attitudes and behaviors. When you need a **moment of Reason** to find the best way to respond to a difficult team situation, say to yourself

> *I am here to be truly helpful.*
>
> *I am here to represent Reason who sent me.*
>
> *I do not have to worry about what to say or what to do because Reason who sent me will direct me.*

When you experience a moment of Reason (a moment of revelation, clarity, or sanity regarding a particular challenge), "remembering" Reason's gentle guidance towards oneness restores your mind to the forgiving Unified Circle of Right-Minded Thinking.

For the full story of Ego's tiny, mad idea of separation and how Reason waits even today to bring us back to oneness, pick up your free copy of the ebook *Reason, Ego & the Right-Minded Teamwork Myth: The Philosophy and Process for Creating a Right-Minded Team That Works Together as One* at RightMindedTeamwork.com or your favorite book retailer. It's also available in paperback.

Reason, Ego & the Right-Minded Teamwork Myth

This book teaches two significant concepts:

- the Right-Minded Teamwork Myth, a short tale that presents RMT's underlying teamwork philosophy of doing no harm and working as one
- the Right-Minded Teamwork team-building tools, methods, and processes to create Right-Minded, productive teams.

The RMT Myth is a short, simple story. It follows three characters: Reason, Ego, and you, the Decision-Maker. Simply put, the RMT Myth and philosophy advocate for teammates to follow Reason's path of oneness instead of following Ego's disastrous advice to seek separateness and prioritize selfishness.

Following the RMT Myth, you will learn about the Right-Minded Teamwork process. Unlike the story, the RMT process is no myth. It is practical, deliberate, and reliable.

The RMT process is a set of interconnected, team-building methods that together form a self-perpetuating, continuous improvement system. This process allows you to integrate the aspirations of the RMT Myth into your team in a way that helps you achieve your business goals.

This book teaches the RMT process and provides a clear overview of the seven other RMT team-building books that, when used together, form a continuous improvement process guaranteed to support team growth and success.

Pick up your free copy at RightMindedTeamwork.com or your favorite book retailer. It is also available in paperback.

Recognition:
Make It Easy to Keep Going

Authentic recognition is not about bestowing company shirts and prizes. It is about giving and receiving genuine appreciation for a job well done.

Recognition plays a critical role in growing your team's business because it keeps your team's spirit ignited. Unfortunately, many people work in team environments where there is little to no recognition. These teammates are discouraged. They do not give their best to the team. Why should they?

Discouraged teammates are like racehorses. If a horse is giving you only 80%, you can whip him, and he will give you 90%. Whip him again, and he will give you 100%. But if you whip him again, after he has already given you everything he has, he will drop back to 80%, or maybe even less. He has learned that you are going to whip him regardless, even if he works harder. So why should he give you his best?

Whipped people leave teams.

Far too often, the ones who leave are the most talented teammates. People that receive legitimate and genuine recognition stay and contribute. Shirts and prizes cannot earn that kind of loyalty or effort.

In the book **Right-Minded Teamwork**: *9 Right Choices for Building a Team That Works as One*, you will learn that Recognition is one of the 9 Right Choices.

See **Critical Few: Complete Important Tasks First**. for a related concept.

Right Choice Model

The *Right Choice Model* is an effective teaching aid that will help you and your teammates choose your own set of unique, "right" teamwork attitudes and behaviors.

Inspired by *A Course in Miracles, The Right Choice Model* consists of two circles. The upper loop of acceptance, forgiveness, and adjustment represents the Unified Circle of Right-Minded Thinking.

The lower loop of rejection, Ego attack, and defensiveness describes the separated or divided circle of wrong-minded thinking.

To learn more about this simple but powerful teaching model, go to RightMindedTeamwork.com or your favorite book retailer, and pick up your copy of *How to Apply the Right Choice Model: Create a Right-Minded Team That Works as One.*

Right-Minded Teamwork's 5-Element Framework

Right-Minded Teamwork is a business-oriented, psychological approach to team building where acceptance, forgiveness, and adjustment are teammate characteristics, and 100% customer satisfaction is the team's result.

Right-Minded Teamwork is built off a framework of 5 Elements consisting of two goals and three teamwork methods.

1. Team **Business Goal**: Achieve 100% Customer Satisfaction
2. Team **Psychological Goal**: Commit to Right-Minded Thinking
3. Team **Work Agreements**: Create & Follow Commitments
4. **Team Operating System**: Make It Effective & Efficient
5. **Right-Minded Teammates**: Strengthen Individual Performance

To learn more, go to RightMindedTeamwork.com or your favorite book retailer, and pick up your copy of ***Right-Minded Teamwork in Any Team***: *The Ultimate Team-Building Method to Create a Team That Works as One.*

Right-Minded Teamwork's 5 Element Implementation Plan

There is no one right way to implement RMT's 5 Element but the three-workshop plan presented in the book *Right-Minded Teamwork in Any Team: The Ultimate Team-Building Method to Create a Team That Works as One* has proven effective countless times.

Here's a brief overview.

First Workshop
Create **psychological goals** plus at least one **Work Agreement**.

Second Workshop
Reaffirm **business goals** and agree on a **team operating system**.

Third Workshop
Encourage and support Right-Minded **Teammate development**.

After the third workshop, and every 90 days after that, you will apply RMT's *Team Operating System & Performance Factor Assessment* to identify opportunities, take action, and achieve new teamwork improvements.

Right-Minded Teamwork
Attitudes & Behaviors

The Right-Minded Teamwork model includes a list of 30 behavioral and process-oriented teammate attitudes and behaviors with their associated costs and benefits. I collected and compiled these over three decades of team-building workshops.

This valuable list includes clear, specific, right, and wrong behaviors "taught" to us by either Reason or Ego.

Thoughts and attitudes always precede teamwork behavior. Right-Minded attitudes come from Reason. Wrong-minded attitudes come from Ego.

The good news is that Right-Minded attitudes are natural. They are already inside you and your teammates. When you think about any of the wrong-minded Ego attitudes listed you will see in the list, ask yourself,

Was I born with these depressing, debilitating, and awful attitudes?

Your answer will always be **"no!"** You learned those wrong-minded attitudes from Ego. That means *you can unlearn them, too*.

You can find the list in several RMT books, including ***How to Apply the Right Choice Model***: *Create a Right-Minded Team That Works as One*, available at RightMindedTeamwork.com or your favorite book retailer.

Right-Mindedness vs. Wrong-Mindedness

"Mindedness" is what you choose to think and perceive. Right-Mindedness refers to the positive mental state, perceptions, choices, and actions you demonstrate when following Reason's guidance.

Wrong mindedness refers to the negative mental state that occurs when you follow Ego's advice.

> *Mindfulness is a journey without distance to a goal **you want to achieve.***

In the book *How to Apply the Right Choice Model: Create a Right-Minded Team That Works as One*, you will find a list of rewards and consequences for choosing Right-Mindedness.

In the book *7 Mindfulness Training Lessons: Improve Teammates' Ability to Work as One with Right-Minded Thinking*, you will learn that in every circumstance, and especially during difficult team situations, Right-Minded Teammates practice mindfulness, or Right-Mindedness, to move them into an ally-focused way of thinking and behaving.

Both of these books will help you accept that your mind is split between two thought systems. At one moment, you are following Reason, and the next, Ego. It is impossible to create and sustain Right-Minded Thinking with a split mind. To heal your split mind, you want to apply the *7 Mindful Training Lessons* and the *Right Choice Model's* attitudes and behaviors.

To bring your team back into the forgiving Unified Circle of Right-Minded Thinking, pick up your copy of these books at your favorite book retailer or RightMindedTeamwork.com.

RMT Motto: Do No Harm. Work as One.

The Right-Minded philosophy is founded on two universal truths:

None of us is as smart as all of us.
Right-Minded Teammates know that working collaboratively together, in a Right-Minded manner, is the only way to create the kind of teamwork that achieves and sustains 100% customer satisfaction. Said differently, these teammates genuinely want and need their fellow teammates.

Do no harm and work as one.
As a Right-Minded Teammate, you can be firm, direct, gentle, and compassionate, all at the same time. You do not blame yourself or others for mistakes. You and your teammates are allies, not adversaries, working together towards your shared goals.

RMT Facilitator

The RMT Facilitator has a special function. Simply put, their expert facilitation *transforms* well-meaning dysfunctional souls into *healthy and functional teammates*.

Using the array of RMT tools, the RMT Facilitator guides teammates in converting their team mistakes into *do-no-harm-work-as-one* attitudes and behaviors.

Teammates are perpetually grateful for the RMT facilitator's help in achieving and sustaining Right-Minded Teamwork. Some even say their RMT Facilitator *saved them.* Team leaders and teammates continually seek the RMT Facilitator's support for years to come.

Team transformations are the RMT Facilitator's **special function**.

Team Management System:
An RMT Enterprise-Wide Process

An enterprise's Team Management System (TMS) aligns all teammate attitudes and work behavior throughout the organization. An effective TMS ensures everyone is doing their part to help the organization achieve the enterprise's vision, mission, and strategic goals.

RMT's Team Management System involves integrating RMT's 5-Element Framework into all teams.

1. Team **Business Goal**: Achieve 100% Customer Satisfaction
2. Team **Psychological Goal**: Commit to Right-Minded Thinking
3. Team **Work Agreements**: Create & Follow Commitments
4. **Team Operating System**: Make It Effective & Efficient
5. **Right-Minded Teammates**: Strengthen Individual Performance

To learn more, go to RightMindedTeamwork.com or your favorite book retailer, and purchase your copy of ***Achieve Your Organization's Strategic Plan****: Create a Right-Minded, Team Management System to Ensure All Teams Work as One.*

Team Operating System & Performance Factor Assessment

RMT's Team Operating System is a six-step, 90-day, continuous improvement operating system that organizes your team functions to increase the likelihood of achieving customer satisfaction.

The system also includes the *Team Performance Factor Assessment* [step 3], which you will use to help teammates identify two to three improvement opportunities every 90 days.

The 25 performance factors in this assessment are aligned with and thus measure the six steps of RMT's Team Operating System. They effectively measure all aspects of Right-Minded Teamwork.

If you want your team to operate more effectively and efficiently, apply this 90-day process after your team has completed the first three RMT workshops. For a brief explanation, see in this glossary: *Right-Minded Teamwork's 5 Element Implementation Plan.*

Apply the three-workshop plan and the operating system, and you nearly guarantee your team will create Right-Minded Teamwork.

To learn the process, go to RightMindedTeamwork.com or your favorite book retailer, and pick up your copy of **Right-Minded Teamwork in Any Team:** *The Ultimate Team-Building Method to Create a Team That Works as One.*

Thought System

<u>What you believe *is* your thought system</u>. Pause and reflect on this truth, and above all, be thankful that it is true.

Whether you are consciously aware of it or not, your thought system is the lens through which you view the world. Without exception, everyone has one. And though there are many variations, there are *only two thought systems* from which to choose:

- A Right-Minded thought system, which extends ally beliefs of acceptance, forgiveness, and adjustment to everyone, everywhere, forever
- A wrong-minded system, which projects adversarial assaults of rejection, attack, and defensiveness to everyone, everywhere, forever

Once you have developed a thought system of any kind, you live it and teach it. Even if you are not entirely aware of it, it remains at the forefront of your mind, influencing your daily behaviors and choices.

If your thought system is negative, or you choose to follow Ego into an unnecessary and adversarial competition, you cannot be a happy, successful teammate.

To live in the land of oneness where your workplace is a safe and supportive classroom and where you and your teammates work as one to achieve team goals, you must train your mind and align your thought system with the teachings of Reason.

There is no possible compromise between these two thought systems. You either collaborate, or you compete. When you follow Ego, you take your team to the battleground. When you choose to follow Reason, you willingly create and genuinely strive to live your team's Work Agreements. With Reason's help, you transform your team into a lovely, collaborative, successful classroom.

The choice is clear.

Reject Ego. Embrace Reason.

Be Thankful.

Train Your Mind

When your mind is well-trained in Reason's Decision-Making ways, Ego attacks do not throw you off course. When a difficult team situation happens, you immediately stop for a **moment of Reason**. You refocus on oneness, rise above the battleground, and remember to live your Work Agreements in your classroom.

To train your mind simply means practicing your team's Work Agreements, which represent your psychological goals, as often as possible, especially during difficult team situations.

Uncovering Root Cause

The Right-Minded Teamwork philosophy advocates leaders, teammates, and facilitators resolve the root cause of teamwork issues instead of making the mistake of addressing symptoms.

Though this view is discussed in many RMT materials, uncovering the root cause is heavily emphasized as a core concept in the book *Design a Right-Minded, Team-Building Workshop: 12 Steps to Create a Team That Works as One*.

Inside that book, you will find a story about a well-meaning team leader who asked me, as their team-building facilitator, if I could teach a three-day workshop in just two days. He believed a quick team event would address the problem he saw in his team.

But the problem he was seeing was only the symptom, not the root cause of the issue. Had I agreed and given him what he asked for, the team would still be struggling with the same issue. And, as a facilitator, I would have failed both the team and the leader.

Instead, by pausing to look for the root cause of the team challenge first, we ended up designing and executing a practical, Right-Minded Teamwork workshop to solve the actual underlying problem.

By seeking out the root cause first, we delivered the leader's desired result, even though the workshop we held was not what he had initially asked for.

To improve your ability to uncover root causes and read this short story, go to your favorite book retailer or RightMindedTeamwork.com and pick up your copy of *Design a Right-Minded, Team-Building Workshop: 12 Steps to Create a Team That Works as One*.

Unified Circle of Right-Minded Thinking

When your team discusses and agrees on your psychological goals – your consciously chosen set of attitudes and behaviors as described in your Work Agreements – you have created your team's collective thought system.

By uniting with each other in this way and openly committing to one another through your Work Agreements, you are renouncing Ego in yourself and your teammates and collectively committing to train your minds to follow Reason.

This process of creating team Work Agreements is your undivided declaration of interdependence. Your assertion is saying,

> *We hold these mindful truths to be self-evident that all minds are created equal, and whosoever believes that will have everlasting freedom to choose Right-Minded Teamwork.*

Your declaration plus your daily acts of living your team Work Agreements *is your return* to the forgiving Unified Circle Right-Minded Thinking.

Work Agreements

A Work Agreement is a collective promise made by teammates to transform non-productive, adversarial behavior into collaborative teamwork behavior. Work Agreements are a key tool for teammates and teams who aspire to do no harm and work as one.

Work Agreements are not flimsy ground rules. They are emotionally mature work performance commitments. Work Agreements announce your dedication to oneness and demonstrate your inner belief that *none of us is as smart as all of us.*

Your team's collective Work Agreements also define your team's psychological goals and thought system. They ensure you conduct your day-to-day work from within your team's Unified Circle of Right-Minded Thinking.

To learn more about the power of Work Agreements and how to use them to transform your team, go to RightMindedTeamwork.com or your favorite book retailer, and pick up your copy of *How to Facilitate Team Work Agreements: A Practical, 10-Step Process for Building a Right-Minded Team That Works as One.*

Resources

To purchase downloadable copies of RMT models and methods to use in your design process, and enroll in this book's online training class, go to RightMindedTeamwork.com, and search for this book's companion *Reusable Resources & Templates*.

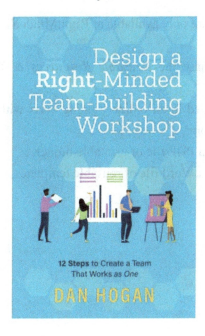

Reusable Resources & Templates

If you purchased the book package from RightMindedTeamwork.com, you were enrolled automatically in an online training class with 2 hours of audio instruction where I share practical concepts and tips on how to apply every step.

You also downloaded reusable templates, checklists, plus a team survey that you could use and reuse.

Online Training Course Plus Reusable Resources & Templates

But if you purchased this book elsewhere, you could also have the training class and reusable material for a special discounted price at RightMindedTeamwork.com.

These materials are only available at RightMindedTeamwork.com

When you purchase the *Reusable Resources & Templates* for this book, you will:
- Be enrolled in an online training class with 2 hours of audio instruction.
- Receive a PDF file of printable models
- Receive a Word file of reusable templates

To Buy these Reusable Resources & Templates

Instructions

1. Go to RightMindedTeamwork.com

2. Reusable Resources tab

Reusable Resources & Templates for Design a Right-Minded Team-Building Workshop

3. Search for ***Reusable Resources & Templates*** for ***Design a Right-Minded Team-Building Workshop:*** *12 Steps to Create a Team That Works as One*

4. Add to Cart to Download

5. Use **Coupon** Code: **12Steps** for 15% off regular price

How to Design a
Right-Minded
TEAMWORK
Team-Building Workshop:
12-Step Process

Right-Minded Teammate Development - 3 Exercises

These three team-building exercises are in the book and this *Reusable Resources & Templates* book. However, the **Defining Teammate Roles and Responsibilities** exercise is downloadable for FREE at RightMindedTeamwork.com.

The Three Exercises

1. Trust Dialogue

The goal of this exercise is to increase and sustain teammates' trust in one another.

2. About Me & My Preferences

The goal of this exercise is to increase teammates' understanding of each other's work preferences. It is much faster than conducting a personality-type-style workshop, and in most cases, it is more effective.

3. Defining Roles and Responsibilities Using 4 Questions

The goal of this exercise is to clarify and define teammate roles and responsibilities using four questions. Doing this will increase your team's likelihood of achieving 100% customer satisfaction.

Trust Dialogue Team-Building Exercise

The Goal

This real-world Trust Dialogue Team-Building Exercise aims to increase and sustain teammates' trust in one another.

This is an effective and impactful exercise. If you are not already an experience team-building facilitator, it is recommended you ask a qualified facilitator to lead this exercise. There is a slight possibility it could upset some teammate relationships rather than improve them.

That said when the workshop is correctly set up and teammates are emotionally and psychologically ready, this exercise, conducted in an all-hands meeting, *will become one of the best team-building practices* you have ever witnessed.

Below is all you need to know for setting up and facilitating this workshop.

Trust Dialogue Outline & Process

At least one week before the workshop, the team leader and facilitator conduct a **Teammate Announcement and Preparation Meeting**.

- There, you will discuss the benefits of increasing and sustaining teammate trust within your team.

- You will also discuss and agree on the desired outcome for the workshop and team-building exercise. (See a sample Agenda below.)

- Everyone at the meeting agrees that all teammates will attend and complete their individual **Teammate Trust Dialogue Preparation Worksheet** before the workshop.

- Teammates understand that their dialogues will be conducted in pairs. Teammates agree to communicate their thoughts and feelings compassionately. Additionally, the dialogues will likely result in the creation of individual or team Work Agreements.
  o Ideally, every teammate will conduct a trust-building dialogue with every other teammate, but there may not be enough time in a single workshop.

- The team leader will decide before the workshop if the teammates are to complete the worksheet on all teammates or narrow it down to specific teammate pairs. If the latter option is chosen, teammates will agree to meet another time to ensure all teammates conduct the trust dialogue.

Teammate Announcement & Preparation Meeting

The team leader and facilitator will co-lead this meeting at least one week before the workshop. They will present and discuss most, if not all, of the following.

- Discuss the benefits of increasing and sustaining teammate trust in your team and why the leader decided to use this exercise and facilitator.

- Present, clarify and agree that all teammates are committed to improving teammate trust.

- Go over how teammates will communicate their thoughts and feelings in their teammate dialogues.

- Remind teammates how to effectively describe trusting behaviors and encourage them to use those behaviors as building blocks for individual or team Work Agreements.

- Next, teammates are instructed on how to complete the **Teammate Trust Dialogue Preparation Worksheet**. See below.

- Eventually, each teammate will create a worksheet for every teammate.

- In this preparation meeting, the team leader will facilitate a short discussion as to what the words **candid**, **listening**, and **partnering** mean. These words and concepts are in the worksheet and the trust dialogue itself.

- Teammates will break out into pairs, sitting face to face. During the workshop's private dialogues, you will share your worksheet information with your teammate.

- One person will share their Trust Dialogue Worksheet information. Clarifying questions will be asked. Understandings are reached. Both teammates will create any needed Work Agreement(s). This first dialogue will take 15 - 20 minutes.

- Next, the second teammate shares their Trust Dialogue Worksheet and repeats the process. Once again, both teammates discuss and create Agreements.

- One round is completed when both teammates have finished their dialogue. It can take as little as 30 minutes to complete one round. Don't rush. But you don't need to talk for an hour.

- After each round, teammates switch partners, then begin the next round.

Team Leader and Facilitator Statements

Here are several statements the leader and facilitator might say during the preparation meeting.

> *All of us want and need to trust one another because we work better together when we trust each other. This exercise will help us increase and sustain our mutual trust.*

> *We will be conducting one-on-one dialogues in an all-hands team workshop on [date]. In those dialogues, you will discuss and agree on how you and your teammates will increase or sustain trust in one another.*

> *The discussion will result in a greater understanding of one another and may result in an individual Work Agreement between two team members or even a team Work Agreement.*

About Trust & Behavior

> *Trust comes from our judgment.*

> *We judge ourselves by our intentions, but we judge others by their behaviors. In this exercise, we will share our intentions and describe behaviors in one-on-one dialogues.*

> *REMEMBER: Be sure you effectively describe work behaviors and not attitudes. A behavior is something you SEE someone do or HEAR what someone says. It is also what they do NOT DO or do NOT SAY.*

An attitude is a judgment. It is not a behavior. However, you may choose to describe a behavior and then say it leads you to a specific attitude or judgment.

Here is a positive example and a negative example. When I arrive at work, you always say hello and ask me how I am doing. You are a really nice person. The "hello" is the behavior, and the "nice person" is the attitude or judgment.

Yesterday, when we were discussing XXX, you raised your voice, and pointed your finger at me, and said, 'Stop talking! You really need to control your anger. The behaviors are "raising your voice" and saying "stop talking." The "control your anger" statement is a judgmental attitude.

In fact, that last statement is an attack, one of the victim steps in the Right Choice Model. We will not make a statement like this in our trust dialogue workshop. Instead, you can say something like this: Yesterday, when we were discussing XXX, you raised your voice, and you pointed your finger at me and said, Stop talking. Maybe I was talking too much, and I think you would agree that raising our voices and pointing fingers will not resolve our conflict or improve trust. Can we find a new way to discuss issues like this in the future?

About Teammate Preparation

*We must come prepared for this exercise. Here is the Trust Dialogue Worksheet. [See Below]. Before the workshop, complete the worksheet on all teammates (or a select sub-group of specific teammates). On the worksheet, you will see three criteria for trust: **candidness**, **listening** and **partnering**.*

***Being candid** means, we are straightforward, forthcoming, and impartial, without pretense or prejudice. It also means we are willing to say we were wrong, which demonstrates our willingness to admit errors in judgment or interpretation.*

***Listening** means tuning in with our whole body and being intentionally emphatic. Listening well is often indicated by rephrasing and reflecting the speaker's ideas, comments, or feelings back to them. One of the most precious gifts we can give one another is the gift of being heard.*

***Partnering** happens when team members feel genuinely supported and encouraged by their teammates. Partnering allows team members to make mistakes and learn from them.*

If we become less candid, don't listen, or distance ourselves from a teammate (not partnering), we lose trust in one another. This Trust Dialogue Exercise will help us avoid these damaging behaviors as we create more collaborative trust within our team.

If we do this exercise well, do you (the team) believe we will improve our trust? And are you willing to do your part as best you can? Typically, team members all say yes to both questions. Their verbal buy-in helps create accountability.

Teammate Trust Dialogue Preparation Worksheet

Instructions: Create one worksheet for every teammate.

Date: _____

My Teammate Partner: _____

My Name: _____

I feel you are ____% **candid** in your communications with me.

I feel ____% **listened** to by you when we speak.

I feel ____% **partnered** with you when we interact.

My Request of my teammate partner

I would be better able or more willing to increase my trust with you if you would (do more, do less, stop/start) this behavior(s): _____

I will also (do more, do less, stop/start) this behavior(s) so as to increase our trust of one another: _____

Our Work Agreement

My teammate partner and I agree to (do more, do less, stop/start) this behavior(s): _____.

My teammate partner and I agree that we will increase our trust in one another if we do this well.

Facilitating Trust Dialogue Workshop

Team Leader and Facilitator Statements

Imagine you are five minutes into your workshop. The team leader has welcomed everyone. All teammates have agreed to the desired outcomes, agenda, ground rules, and logistics.

Consider taking a few more moments, perhaps five minutes, to introduce the **Right Choice Model**. Your goal is to present the Model in such a way that when you finish teaching it, all teammates declare,

> *Of course, we want to approach this trust dialogue exercise in a Right-Minded, accountable way. Let's get started.*

To learn about the Right Choice Model, go to RightMindedTeamwork.com or your favorite book retailer, and pick up ***How to Apply the Right Choice Model***: *Create a Right-Minded Team That Works as One*. Look for the section titled: How to Present & Apply the Right Choice Model in Your Team. In that book, you will be given specific instructions on how to present the model successfully.

Here are several additional comments the leader and facilitator could share at the beginning of the workshop.

> *The dialogues you have today will help our team increase and sustain trust.*
>
> *Your dialogues will increase your understanding of one another and will result in new Work Agreements.*
>
> *When you say to your teammate that you could increase your trust in them if they did this or that, be sure to describe behaviors and not attitudes and ask if they would be willing to honor your request. If they say yes, you must allow them to ask you clarifying questions.*
>
> *No matter what, do not get defensive. Use reflective listening such as saying, 'So what I hear you saying is ____. Did I get it right?*

Advocate, Inquire/Ask, Disagree

Here are some additional phrases you may use to help create a positive trust dialogue between yourselves.

To **Advocate** for something, say:

> *Here's what I'm thinking and how I got there...*
> *Some of the assumptions I've made are...*
> *I reached the conclusion I did because...*
> *Here's who will be affected by my request, how they will be affected, and why...*

To **Inquire** or **Ask,** say

> *What data are you using to reach that conclusion?*
> *What's leading you to make that conclusion?*
> *What would this mean to...?*
> *Can you give me an example?*

When you **Disagree,** say

> *Tell me again how you came to believe this point of view.*
> *Are you using any data I may not have considered?*
> *Am I understanding correctly, what you're saying...?*
> *I'm having difficulty with "X", because of this reasoning...*

Trust Dialogue Meeting Agenda

Desired Outcome: Building Teammate Trust

Agenda
- Kick-off: Agree on the Desired Outcome
- Dialogue Instructions & Group Discussion
- Breakout in pairs for Round #1
- Breakout for Round #2
- Round #3
- Reconvene & Debrief as a full team
- Close

About Me & My Preferences
Team-Building Exercise

These three exercises are in this book's companion *Reusable Resources & Templates* book that you may purchase and download only at RightMindedTeamwork.com. However, the **Defining Teammate Roles and Responsibilities** exercise is downloadable for FREE at RightMindedTeamwork.com.

The Goal

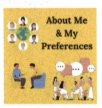

The goal of this real-world **About Me & My Preferences Team-Building Exercise** is to increase teammates' understanding of each other's work preferences.

I used this exercise many times in my team-building practice. It was a wildly successful exercise. It never failed. And it is much faster than conducting a personality-type-style workshop.

In most cases, it was actually more effective than personality workshops because teammates address their most important work preferences. Doing that means they can create meaningful **Work Agreements** to build and sustain Right-Minded Teamwork.

Do this exercise, and you will be following Reason's Right-Minded Teamwork philosophy of **Do No Harm** and **Work as One**.

Exercise Instructions

- Teammates choose one, maybe two, of the questions below to answer.
- They bring their answers to a **team meeting that all teammates attend.**
- Each teammate shares at least one answer.
- Other teammates ask clarifying questions.
- If appropriate, the team or individual teammates will create Work Agreements to resolve identified challenges.
- IMPORTANT: Conduct this conversation in a collaborative and compassionate spirit. Find ways to work with another's preferences. Do not try to change another teammate.
- Remember: Right-Minded Teammates do no harm and work as one.

Preferences Exercise Questions

1. How would you describe your work style? What works or does not work well when it comes to interacting with you and your work style?
2. If another teammate thinks you are about to make a mistake, what is the best way for them to respond or call it to your attention? And what will be your responsibility?
3. What is the best way for others to express disagreement or alternative opinions without offending you? And what will be your responsibility if they don't?
4. What are your pet peeves? What makes you mad? If you are triggered, what is the best way for you and the other person to recover?
5. The biggest mistake another teammate can make with me is _____, and the best way we can recover is _____.
6. The best way to communicate with me is _____, and the best way to motivate me is _____.

Defining Teammate Roles and Responsibilities Exercise Using 4 Questions

These three exercises are in this book's companion *Reusable Resources & Templates* book that you may purchase and download only at RightMindedTeamwork.com. However, this exercise, **Defining Teammate Roles and Responsibilities,** is downloadable for FREE at RightMindedTeamwork.com.

The Goal

Defining teammate roles and responsibilities using these four questions will increase your team's likelihood of achieving 100% customer satisfaction.

Many teams go off the rails because they don't know how to define and clarify teammate roles and responsibilities, or they simply don't take the time to make them clear.

Certainly, it doesn't have to be that way.

Sustainability

Clarifying teammate roles is a sure way to sustain high-performance teamwork, and this four-question roles and responsibilities workshop is faster and better than creating a RACI Matrix.

Similarly, as preventive maintenance ensures your car runs properly, conducting a periodic team-building workshop to re-clarify teammate roles and responsibilities will do the same for your team.

Why Clarify Teammate Roles?

If you don't perform "maintenance," teammates will start acting like an old, clunky car. Without clarity, they burn oil and blow smoke.

Periodic role calibration ensures your team is focused on doing the right things right. Conducting this exercise in a team meeting or team-building workshop will allow you to:

- Ensure everyone understands and accepts their role, responsibility, and accountability.

- Give positive appreciation to team members for providing resources and support so other teammates may meet or exceed their responsibilities.

- Modify and agree on new and better ways to execute individual roles within the team.

Teammate Preparation

To prepare for this exercise, teammates will answer four questions:

1. Name the **top three key** deliverables, objectives, or products you produce for the team.

2. What resources or support do you need that **you are currently receiving?**

3. What resources or support do you need that you **are not currently receiving?**

4. What are **you getting that you don't need**? What is hurting your performance?

Teammates should be prepared to offer positive changes and suggestions to improve their role as well as the roles of others.

They should also be ready to provide solutions as to how they can get what they need or how they can let go of what they don't need.

Leader's Guide

Before the meeting, the team leader:

1. Sets a date for the exercise and invites all team members.

2. Let all team members know participation is required.

3. Distribute questions to teammates one to two weeks before the workshop date.

4. Asks teammates to write their answers to all four questions.

5. Print copies of those answers and distribute them to teammates in the workshop.

6. Ask teammates to review their answers before the workshop and to come prepared to discuss and agree with fellow teammates.

7. Ask teammates to watch this six-minute video. Dan will explain the Roles Exercise and discuss the importance of an attitude of teammate Oneness. Go to RightMindedTeamwork.com. Search for *"Define Teammate Roles Responsibilities with just four questions."*

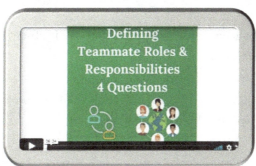

During the meeting, the team leader or facilitator:

1. Presents workshop outcomes and invites teammates to agree.

2. Ensures all teammates understand the goal of exercise. (An excellent way to do this is to ask a teammate to explain it, then allow others to comment.)

3. Obtains agreement that clear roles and responsibilities will help ensure they work and behave as one unified team.

4. Presents group exercise instructions:
   - One teammate will give their answers to all four questions, without interruption, in one to two minutes.
   - Open dialogue will follow to validate and constructively challenge their views.
   - That teammate will enjoy receiving appreciation from fellow teammates.
   - All will agree on how their teammate will get what they need or let go of what they don't need.
   - The team will document all key agreements and understandings.
   - When the first teammate discussion is complete, the second teammate will give their answers.

5. Keeps teammates engaged (so no one is absent or brushes off the activity).

6. Help the team agree on how they will track progress and when they will recalibrate team roles again.

7. Schedules a second meeting to complete the exercise if time runs short.

After the meeting:

1. At the next few team meetings, the team leader asks all teammates, "Are we honoring and following our agreed-upon roles and responsibilities?"

Role Clarification Meeting Agenda

Desired Outcome: Discuss, clarify, confirm, and agree on who does what, when, and how.

Time Commitment: 2-4 hours

Participants:7 teammates

Agenda
A. Kick-off
B. Agree on the Desired Outcome
C. Agree to believe and behave as one unified team
D. RMT's Role Clarification exercise
   - One person at a time gives answers to the questions.
   - Dialogue follows.
   - Time permitting, create new Work Agreements & teammate understandings
   - Capture conclusions in the Team Business Plan.
   - If you run out of time, complete as many as possible, then schedule a second session to continue.
E. Close

Benefits of Ongoing Feedback

Goals + Feedback = Success

Goals give people direction, and clear roles and responsibilities are a form of goals. But goals alone aren't enough. The following study shows how feedback can make a tough goal to feel more achievable. It illustrates the practical logic of providing ongoing, clear feedback.

A group of soldiers endured weeks of arduous training to qualify for elite combat units. At the end of the training, a final challenge remained: a forced march in full gear.

The soldiers were divided into four groups. Each group would march 20 kilometers (about 13 miles) over exactly the same terrain on the same day. The only variation was that each group received different instructions.

The first group was told, "You'll march 20 kilometers" (the actual distance). These soldiers received regular progress reports along the route.

The second group was given less information: "This is the long march you heard about." Group members didn't know how far they would march, nor were they informed of their progress along the way.

The third group was given an underestimation: "You'll march 15 kilometers." But after marching 14 kilometers, they were told they had six more to go.

The fourth and final group received an overestimation: "You'll march 25 kilometers." After marching 14, they were told they had only six more to go.

The results were clear. Researchers found that the first group performed the best. Knowing how far they were going and receiving regular progress reports helped the soldiers complete the 20-kilometer course the fastest, with the least stress.

Group two had the slowest time and endured more stress than all the other groups. With no idea how far they were going - only that it was a "long march" - and no feedback on their progress, group two's morale and performance suffered.

Interestingly, though groups three and four received incorrect feedback, they still outperformed group two.

Apparently, any feedback improves morale.

Source: *Encouraging The Heart, James M. Kouzes, and Barry Z. Posner, Jossey Bass Publishers, 350 Sansome St. San Francisco, CA 94104*

Whether entirely accurate or not, feedback tells team members they're making progress toward goals and are living up to expectations. It reminds them someone cares enough about them to keep them informed.

More About Roles: The RACI Matrix

For a more detailed and complex role exercise, try the Responsibility Assignment Matrix. It is a powerful tool for clarifying the way team members work together.

I facilitated many RACI's in my career. The following RACI chart was used to define the responsibilities of all employees involved in a plant operations maintenance process.

Sometimes, this model is called RACI, which stands for:

R = Responsible

A = Accountable

C = Consulted

I = Informed

	Maintenance Management Process	Create Work Orders	Plan WOs	Approval	Procure Material	Receive Material	Schedule WOs	Assign Work	Prepare Equipment & Permits	Complete Work	Safety Activities	Maintenance Reports	Cost Control/Budget Preparations	RCFAs	RCM Analysis	MOCs	PMs	PM Job Plans	PdM Data Collection	PdM Data Analysis	CBM Action Item WOs
RC Manager	A	R	C	A	C		R	I	I		R/A	R/A	R/A	A	A	R	A	I	A	C/I	A
Maintenance Engineer	R	R	R	R	R	I	R	I	I	R/A	R	R	R	R	R	R	R	R		R	R
Reliability Engineer	R	R	C		C		I	I		C	R	I	C	R	R	R	R	R/A	R	R/A	R
Maintenance Planner	R		R/A	I	R/A	R	C				R	I	R			R	R	C			R
Maintenance Scheduler	R	R	I	I	I	A	R/A	R	I		R	R	R			C/I	R	C	R		C
Maintenance Coordinator	R	R	R	I	R	R	C	R/A	R	R	R	I	R	C		C/I	R	C	R		R
Maintenance Specialist	R	R	R		R	R	I	I	I	I	R	R	C	R	C	C	C	C	C		C
Production Tech	R	R					C/I		R	C/I		I		C/I	C/I						
Plant Manager	R	R/A	C/I	R	C/I		R	I	A	C/I	R	I	R	C/I	R	A	R	I	R	I	R

5 Keys to Proper Communication

The way you talk and interact with your team leader and teammates will help you understand the team's issues.

Why? Because intentional interaction creates trust and confidence. And the more they trust you, the more open and honest they will be with you.

Here are five keys to proper communication:

1. Reflect their answers

When you do well, reflecting the team's comments back to them, they will believe you understand their needs better than they do. This mindset allows them to receive your facilitation, feedback, and suggestions positively.

Reflecting answers is not hard. But it does take consistent practice.

2. Create safety

You may sometimes find teammates are apprehensive about talking with you. They might feel embarrassed, or they may view themselves as less-than-competent.

Reassure concerned or apprehensive teammates by telling them your team facilitation support is a positive indication that the leader genuinely cares about them.

In the end, teammates will respect the leader even more.

3. Start with open-ended questions

Open-ended questions encourage discussion. If you're unsure where to start, you can use some of the questions from the **9 Right Choices Survey** in the Right-Minded Teamwork book, such as:

- Do all team members understand the team's vision?
- Has the team created practical Work Agreements?
- Do teammates look for ways to correct mistakes and resolve conflicts?

4. Probe

There is always more to a story or situation than the first version shared. Ask clarifying questions to learn more. As you probe, be incredibly careful not to express judgment or evaluation through your body language or tone of voice.

5. Engage teammates through accountability and commitment

After hearing about the team's potential outcomes, ask questions that help establish accountability and commitment. You could ask, "Are you willing to do your part in helping your teammates achieve those outcomes?"

14 Characteristics of a
Successful RMT Team Building Facilitator

Friendly	Gentle	Playful
Collaborative	Outcome-Driven	Engaging
Attentive	Helpful	Non-Judgmental
Facilitative	Practical	Self-Reflecting
Focused	Mature	

Every facilitator brings their own personality and flair to their facilitation work, but successful facilitators share these key characteristics.

Friendly
The facilitator sets the tone for the workshop. When teammates walk in feeling welcomed and excited to be there, the facilitator has played a key role in creating that atmosphere. With the best facilitators, you feel like you're being welcomed into their home.

Collaborative
Facilitators use their body language, tone of voice, and word choice to support workshop outcomes. They also use their environment strategically.

By setting the tone and carefully arranging the room, facilitators can create a professional yet comfortable atmosphere that encourages real discussion amongst all teammates. This air of active involvement creates a collaborative learning environment.

Attentive
An effective facilitator continually practices seeing, hearing, and feeling the interpersonal dynamics in the room. They watch body language and listen to the tone of voice, looking for patterns. They also observe how listeners react to other speakers' information.

Facilitative
It may sound obvious, but good facilitators know how to use facilitative tools. They realize using these tools is the "means" and not the "end," so they do not overuse them. Rather than attempting to facilitate the process perfectly, they maintain focus on achieving the meeting outcome(s).

Focused
Excellent facilitators stay one mental step ahead of participants. They continually ask themselves, "What's next on the agenda?" and "How will we get from here to the desired outcome and beyond?" They bring strategic thinking and strategic facilitation into their workshops.

Gentle
When there's tension or conflict in the room, effective facilitators don't avoid the problem. Instead, they gently move towards it. They "do no harm" to everyone.

They look at the choices being made by participants. They listen for key points and reflect them back. They are skilled at summarizing. They know how to carefully reflect a situation so participants can see the problem clearly and recognize the necessity for addressing it.

Outcome-Driven

Strong facilitators use the workshop agenda, particularly the meeting's desired outcome, to keep the discussions on track. They keep the outcome firmly implanted in their minds, and they use it as a filter to screen teammate communication.

They constantly ask themselves how the current discussion relates to the overall desired outcome. If it relates, they stay out of the way and let the participants do their work. If the conversation goes off track, they interrupt and ask, "How does this information help achieve our desired outcome?"

Helpful

Instead of asking people to accept the meeting's desired outcomes blindly, good facilitators help participants identify "what's in it for them." Then, they synergize the teammates' motivations to align with the desired meeting outcomes. For important meetings, this work is done before the meeting, not during.

Practical

Successful facilitators know there are two kinds of barriers: processes and people. While planning an important meeting, successful facilitators proactively ask themselves what could go wrong. They identify specific barriers within the team, and they plan ways to prevent these barriers from arising. They also plan how they will intervene if their preventions don't work.

Mature

The most effective facilitators are true to themselves. They know there is no one right way to facilitate. They don't try to mimic other successful facilitators; they find their own voice. They improve and grow their personal facilitation style.

Playful

Facilitators may be humorous, but they never use humor at anyone's expense.

Engaging

Good facilitators look for and take advantage of opportunities to get participants moving. Often, this means getting participants to do something with their entire bodies, not just their minds.

Non-Judgmental

Effective facilitators don't have to be neutral. But they do have to be willing to step aside from their own beliefs and values in order to facilitate objectively. They know how to share their opinions without directing, and regardless of their views, they offer their critical-thinking skills to help the group make the best decision.

Self-Reflecting

Successful facilitators ask themselves these honest questions:

- Do I understand the outcome from the stakeholders' perspectives?
- Have I done my homework, and am I prepared for the unexpected?
- If people get upset or things seem to go wrong in the meeting, do I have a predetermined set of values and principles to guide my choices and interactions?

When a facilitator can answer yes to these questions, they know they're ready.

1st Draft Team Building Workshop Plan
Agenda & Punch List

To: Team Leader
From: [You, the Facilitator]
Date:
Subject: 1st Draft Team Building Plan

This is the 1st Draft Plan for our team building workshop, and it includes:

1. Outcomes & Agenda
2. Punch List
3. Announcement copy (In the Resources, see "Announcing Workshop via Email - a Template" for a sample copy to share with the team leader)

After we discuss this plan on _____ (date), our next steps will be:

- Conduct and compile the result of the Right-Minded Teammate survey.
- With the survey information, I will conduct individual teammate interviews.
- After the interviews, I will create a 2nd Draft Plan.
- Then, I will report back to you on _____ (date) to finalize the workshop outcomes and agenda.

Below/attached, you will find the 1st Draft Agenda (including workshop Outcomes); the initial Punch List follows.

Lastly, I'll provide you with a sample email for announcing the workshop.

Punch List

If two or more teammates brought up a topic, issue, challenge and / or conflict in the facilitator interviews, the essence is captured in question format and added to this list.

Note to facilitators: This template is for the initial Punch List, created after the initial team leader interview. This document is a work in progress that will be expanded after you interview teammates. You will present an updated version of the Punch List in Step #9 as part of the 2nd Draft Plan.

A. Meeting Effectiveness & Communications

1. What does open, honest, and straightforward communication look like within our team?
2. How can we make our meetings more effective and less confrontational?
3. If someone approaches you about their difficulty with your communication style, what should you do?
4. If someone comes to you and complains about another team member / leader, what should you do?
5. If you continue to hear the same basic complaints from the same people, what should you do?

1st Draft Agenda

<table>
<tr>
<td rowspan="2"></td>
<td>Team Building Workshop – 1ST Draft
Date:
Time:
Location:</td>
</tr>
<tr>
<td></td>
</tr>
<tr>
<td align="right">Attendees</td>
<td></td>
</tr>
<tr>
<td align="right">Please Read</td>
<td><ul><li>The Punch List below</li><li>Think about and create specific suggestions as to how to improve/fix/correct/etc. Punch List items, especially ____</li></ul></td>
</tr>
<tr>
<td align="right">Please Bring</td>
<td></td>
</tr>
<tr>
<td colspan="2" align="center">Purpose & Desired Outcomes</td>
</tr>
<tr>
<td colspan="2">

Purpose: To create and sustain high-performance teamwork

Desired Outcomes
1. Discuss and agree on how to improve **meeting effectiveness**
2. Discuss and agree on how to improve **team communications**
3. Other?

</td>
</tr>
</table>

Agenda		
What	Who	When
1. Welcome & Kick-Off • Share purpose, the desired outcome • Review agenda, meeting behaviors, & agreements	Team Leader, Facilitator	10 -15 min
2. Meeting Effectiveness & Communications • Discuss & agree on how to improve • Solve the problem / create a Work Agreement		
3. FIRST Punch List Topic • Define the problem • Solve the problem / create a Work Agreement		
4. SECOND Punch list Topic • Define the problem • Solve the problem / create a Work Agreement		
5. Closure: • Agree on how / when to resolve other Punch List topics • List workshop positives as well as things to do differently in the next workshop • Review & commit to Agreements and/or Action Plan • Acknowledgments & appreciations		

2nd Draft Team Building Workshop Plan
Agenda & Punch List

To: Team Leader

From: [You, the Facilitator]

Date:

Subject: 2nd Draft Team Building Plan

This is the 2nd Draft Plan, and it includes:

1. Outcomes & Agenda: a new and more detailed version

2. Punch List: a summarization of challenges based on teammate interviews

3. RMT survey results

4. Suggestions for:

   - creating preventions & interventions

   - how to distribute the agenda to all teammates

2nd Draft Agenda

	Team Building Workshop – *2nd Draft* Date: Time: Location:
Attendees	
Please Read	• The Punch List below • Think about and create specific suggestions as to how to improve/fix/correct/etc. Punch List items, especially _____
Please Bring	

Purpose & Desired Outcomes

Purpose: To create and sustain high-performance teamwork

Desired Outcomes

1. Discuss and agree on how to improve **meeting effectiveness**
2. Discuss and agree on how to improve **team communications**
3. Discuss and agree on how to improve **work ethics** so as to increase openness, trust, respect, and efficiency in our team.
4. Agree on how and when to address **customer satisfaction** and **roles & responsibilities**

Agenda		
What	Who	When

1. Welcome & Kick-Off
  • Share purpose, the desired outcome
  • Review agenda, meeting behaviors, & agreements
	Team Leader, Facilitator	10 -15 min

2. **Meeting Effectiveness**
  • Discuss & agree on how to improve
  • Solve the problem / create a Work Agreement		

3. **Team Communications**
  • Define the problem
  • Solve the problem / create a Work Agreement		

4. NEXT Punch list Topic
  • Define the problem
  • Solve the problem / create a Work Agreement		

5. Closure:
  • Agree on how / when to resolve other Punch List topics
  • List workshop positives as well as things to do differently in the next workshop
  • Review & commit to Agreements and/or Action Plan
  • Acknowledgments & appreciations		

Punch List

If two or more teammates brought up a topic, issue, challenge and / or conflict in the facilitator interviews, the essence was captured in a question format and added to this list.

NOTE: Below is a sample of a final Punch List (from Step 8). This is an actual Punch List from a RMT workshop I facilitated. Use it as a guide. Remember this is a final draft; the initial draft did not have this much detail.

A. Meeting Effectiveness & Communication

1. Many people said they want open, honest, and straightforward communication; what does that look like?
2. Is it OK to use toxic / inflammatory words, tone or body language? When you slip and use toxic communication, and you realize you wish you had not, what should you do? What is an appropriate apology?
3. If someone approaches you about their difficulty with your communication style, what should you do?
4. If someone comes to you and complains about another team member / leader, what should you do? If you continue to hear the same basic complaints from the same people, what should you do?

B. Work Ethic

This is about – interaction style, conflict resolution, work quality, productivity, interdependency, etc. - that increases trust, respect and confidence in one another.

1. Is it OK to have an unresolved conflict if it affects individual and / or team productivity? If not, what is our work agreement regarding solving conflicts and / or giving performance feedback? For instance…
2. If someone doesn't do what they said they'd do (or are assigned to do) how do you call it out in a supportive way? How do you hold them accountable?
3. If a teammate doesn't perform like you believe they should, what should you do? For instance, if you believe another person should perform a particular responsibility, is it OK to call it out?
4. Trust & respect…if you do not trust another person and it affects your performance, what should you do?
5. If we feel we are not getting acknowledged / recognized for our work, what should we do?

C. Customer Satisfaction

1. Are we giving our customers both internal and external exceptional service?
2. Do we know for certain our customers believe we're giving them exceptional service? If yes, how? If no, why not?
3. Do we listen to our customers and give them what they need? If we do, then they are very excited about paying our department's budget – right?
4. Do our customers know our capabilities as well as we do? If no, why not? How do we / should we educate our customers?

D. Roles & Responsibilities

1. Who in our team is primarily responsible for customer relations and satisfaction? How do they ensure we are creating and sustaining an incredibly good relationship with them?
2. For those who have key responsibilities, what are the 3-5 key behaviors and / or results they need to demonstrate for our team? What support do they need from others in our department?
3. When you ask to perform a particular task, and you do not understand, agree with or feel it is your role and responsibility, what should you do? How should you question it?
4. Is everyone clear and in agreement with how decisions are made in our team?
5. Where are duplicate work efforts and how can we streamline those work processes?

Announcing Workshop via Email - a Template

To: Teammates
CC: You - the Facilitator
From: Team Leader
Subject: Team Building Workshop Date: __/__/____

As you know, we have agreed to take part in a team-building workshop.

To facilitate our workshop, I'm very pleased to announce I have retained _____ (you, the Facilitator) who comes highly recommended by _____.

I have had several calls with _____ (you, the Facilitator), and this workshop announcement outlines how you, I, and _____ (you, the Facilitator) will work together to design a workshop that addresses our needs.

This will be a customized team building workshop. It is based on teamwork principles from a method called Right-Minded Teamwork.

This is not a training program, nor will we be playing team games. We will, instead, work on our real teamwork issues. That is what I want to talk about with you.

Please hear this: Our team, in many ways, performs very well. And we've also agreed we can and want to improve our performance.

Currently, I think this workshop will be a two-day event. I've tentatively scheduled it for _____ (dates). Please hold those dates on your calendar. When we finalize the workshop outcomes in about two weeks, we will decide if it is a one or two-day event.

As I said, I have spoken to _____ (you, the Facilitator), and I have shared my outcome ideas. Here are two workshop outcomes I am putting forward:

1. Discuss and agree on how to improve meeting effectiveness
2. Discuss and agree on how to improve team communications

_____ (you, the Facilitator) took my ideas and created a 1st Draft Plan. However, we both agreed it is essential for all teammates to participate in creating the team building workshop outcomes.

Here are the steps we'll take to make that happen.

1. I want you to read this short book because it will help us identify what is important and create a common language.
   - The book is ***Right-Minded Teamwork****: 9 Choices for Building a Team that Works... As One.*
   - It will take you less than 30 minutes to read it.

2. Next, we will all complete a teammate survey and give our answers to _____ (you, the Facilitator).
   - (You can either use the RMT 9 Right Choices survey or the RMT 20-Question Team Perception Survey.)

3. After everyone has completed the survey, _____ (you, the Facilitator) will interview each teammate and share our survey results.

4. When _____ (you, the Facilitator) finishes the interviews, _____ (you, the Facilitator) will create a 2nd Draft Plan for the workshop and report back to me. The Plan will include:
   - A new and refined list of outcomes
   - A detailed agenda along with custom exercises to help us achieve those outcomes
   - A master Punch List, which summaries all the teamwork topics and issues we collectively want to address over time

5. _____ (you, the Facilitator) and I will discuss and eventually finalize that Plan. Afterward, we will distribute the final agenda to you.

How does this sound to you?

I look forward to working with you.

Sincerely,
Team Leader

Another Root Cause Story

What the team leader asks for isn't always what they need!

One summer, I received a call from a potential new customer. He was a partner-in-charge of an architectural design firm.

He asked, "Can you facilitate one of those off-site meetings you do?"

"Yes," I said. "What do you want to accomplish?"

He said he wanted to increase trust and get the other founding partner to change his work behavior.

As it turned out, the other founding partner was driving everyone crazy. He was making customers angry. He was even running off some of their best employees.

In general, my prospective client wanted his partner to stop all the whining and complaining. The team was having their best year ever, and he didn't want to blow it!

He went on to say, "We need to talk about this issue in an offsite meeting. We need to resolve it and move on. I just don't have time for all this dysfunctional behavior!"

"Okay," I said. "I need to interview all the principals before we design a draft agenda for this offsite meeting." He gave me the green light, and we moved ahead.

What I heard in the interviews validated the head partner's perception: There was a lack of trust, and the leaders were very frustrated with the other founding partner. Most believed that if he were gone, all the problems would be solved.

What I learned in the interviews was the organization had very little team and organizational structure. They had no strategic plan and no team operating system. In addition to those complaints about the other founding partner, everyone on the team agreed they needed a cohesive vision and more structure.

I reported back to the head partner and reflected what I was seeing.

I said, "Sometimes, the best way to address dysfunctional behavior is to resolve work process issues. I recommend that in the offsite meeting, we create the organization's first strategic plan and operating structure. Once that is in place if a particular leader or partner doesn't do their part, then you can easily implement corrective action or termination."

The head partner agreed to the plan.

A few weeks later, I facilitated the offsite with fantastic results:

- The team created their first strategic plan with five clear, measurable, strategic goals.

- A week after the offsite, they conducted an all-employee survey to assess where they stood relative to those five goals.

- Given the opportunity, the other founding partner did not change his attitude or behavior. So, the head partner had to make a difficult decision, and the other founding partner was forced into retirement.

- Trust among the partners, and other leaders steadily increased over the next year.

- The company now has a strategic planning process they will repeat every year going forward.

Initially, the head partner asked for help to increase trust and for his co-founder to change his behavior.

Had I facilitated a meeting focused on increasing trust and dealing with bad behavior, I would have given the partner what he initially wanted... but not what was actually needed.

Instead, we implemented what the team and the organization needed: a strategic plan and a strong team structure.

Even though what I provided was not what he asked for, within six months, the head partner achieved everything he wanted.

Maria's Effective Workshop Close

The Work Agreements workshop James had been facilitating was about to end.

Maria, the team leader, turned to him in front of the ten other team members and said, "Thank you very much! We could not have been this successful without you."

The entire team gave James a round of applause. He smiled and communicated his deep appreciation by meeting the eyes of each team member. He said nothing.

James was joyful. Here was one more positive experience that validated his team-building facilitation skills. It was yet another confirmation he'd made the right choice to follow a real-world team-building approach.

Years earlier, James had become dissatisfied with the team-building tools he'd been using. They were not working as well as he thought they should. He knew there had to be a better way to build and sustain collaborative teams, so he began searching for one.

Then, a colleague from another organization told him about the Work Agreement approach. The team had been using it for several months and was delighted with the results. James knew immediately it was the solution he'd been looking for.

As he immersed himself in the new approach, James quickly understood how creating Work Agreements for teams was a simple yet effective concept. But James had facilitated enough events to know there would be some who'd consider the concept too elementary. Those misguided folks would argue their simplicity was proof that Work Agreements wouldn't work.

But now, James had personal evidence of their effectiveness.

Maria went on to tell her team that although the last two days had not been easy, they'd been well worth the work the team had put in. She shared that even though they'd addressed some difficult subjects (such as learning to respect one another's feelings and opinions), she was confident that the Agreements, understandings, and decisions the team had created together would help ensure they reached and sustained higher levels of future performance.

Next, Maria announced the work they had begun would continue with two additional team-building workshops, with James as their facilitator.

The second workshop would be held in four to five weeks. In that workshop, they would create and install a self-sustaining, continuous-improvement team operating system. Then the third workshop would be conducted six to seven months later and would focus on "Right-Minded Team Players Who Act as One."

She also announced that the team would begin mandatory staff meetings every Tuesday morning starting in two weeks. They would continue weekly for an extended period of time, and then they would be held every other week.

Then Maria did something wonderful that genuinely surprised her team: She went around the room and briefly gave a special, heartfelt thank you to each team member for his or her positive contribution to the Work Agreements workshop's success.

After a few appreciative replies and comments from team members that validated Maria's statements, she adjourned the meeting.

She walked over to where James was waiting. Maria again expressed her appreciation, and he was able to return the compliment. He gave her positive feedback about the way the two of them had partnered in planning and facilitating the workshop.

James said, "After I completed the team member interviews two weeks ago, I realized how right you were. It was important to you that teammates discuss and resolve their issues, especially the lack of respect issue. You could have told them what to do. But you demonstrated true collaborative leadership by setting it up so that they created their own solutions."

Maria smiled. James knew she understood the power behind having team members make their own Work Agreements because they'd be more likely to live and follow them after the workshop. While most team leaders know this to be true, James had seen even well-meaning leaders skip this important step.

James went on, "I have worked with many leaders over the years. You did one of the best jobs of preparing your team members I have ever seen. By speaking with each one last week, you were able to lower their anxieties and increase their readiness to address issues. You must have been successful in mitigating their fears because they were ready to talk!"

Maria smiled with gratitude for the praise, and James continued.

"I'm also glad you, and I discussed how we would interact if the conversation became toxic. Even though there were no nasty attacks, some people, like George and Linda, received some difficult messages. I really appreciated the way you let me take the lead to facilitate their efforts toward accountability. I especially liked how you took my comments and reinforced them.

"Specifically, you said, 'We need to be respectfully honest with each other, especially if it helps our team meet or exceed our mission.' I also appreciated it when you told the team, 'It is okay to disagree with one another and with me, but it's not okay to behave in a disagreeable manner.'"

Maria replied, "Thanks. I was grateful that you were able to facilitate the conversation because it gave me time to consider how I should respond. I think we were a good pair, and I'm convinced the Work Agreements our team made will work. But I know that we have to live and follow them. I will do my part by conducting those Agreement review moments at the beginning of our weekly staff meetings, as you suggested."

After exchanging a few brief words with other team members, James tidied up the meeting room, packed his materials, and headed home, satisfaction filling his heart.

Meeting Plan Checklist

Purpose of the Meeting _____

Desired Outcomes

    1. ABC

    2. XYZ

Stakeholders:

- Participants in meeting: What's in it for them?
- Non-participants: What's in it for them?
- What do participants need to do to prepare?

Decision-Making Work Agreement & fallback _____

Barriers to this meeting

- Processes Barriers
- People Barriers

Preventions & Interventions to the Barriers _____

Roles & Responsibilities

- Facilitator: _____
- Scribe: _____
- Timekeeper: _____
- Sponsors: _____
- Others: _____

Room Arrangement & other logistics_____

Meeting Notes & Distribution _____

Follow-up Strategies & Action Items _____

More Facilitator Interview Questions

Teammate interviews are always conducted one-on-one, either in person or over the phone.

In many cases, you will want to interview every team member. For teams or departments with over thirty people, it is acceptable to interview a representative sample.

The interview questions you choose should help you achieve the leader's desired outcomes.

For example, if the leader wants to increase productivity and profits, you will ask more questions about the team's vision, roles, and responsibilities.

If they want to know what is needed to improve morale, you will ask more questions about the team's interpersonal relationships.

In either case, you will ask a series of questions in order to identify the team's performance barriers.

A balanced set of interview questions can cover a multitude of topics. Take some time to design the best set of questions you can.

Before you begin asking questions, make sure you let your interviewee know what they share with you is confidential; however, you will summarize their collective comments in a Punch List, with no attribution.

Possible Interview Questions

1. Do you understand the organization's vision, mission, and strategic objectives?

2. To what degree are the team's vision, mission, and strategic objectives clear and understood? How does the team vision support the organization?

3. Is the team achieving or exceeding goals in these four business-outcome areas?
   - Financial performance
   - Product & service quality
   - Work process efficiencies
   - Human development

4. Are all team members clear about their roles, responsibilities, and accountabilities?

5. Does the team have productive team meetings and team decision-making processes?

6. Is the current leadership style the best for this group?

7. To what degree does the team communicate effectively?

8. How are team relationships? Is there trust, support, and respect for one another?

9. To what degree is the team able to focus and follow through on the critical-few work projects?

10. To what degree does the team correct and learn from mistakes?

11. Does the team have a continuous-improvement process in place, and is it consistently implemented?

12. To what degree does the team recognize and acknowledge fellow team members?

13. What do you think about the leader's desired workshop outcomes? Are they of value to you? If no, what would be of greater value?

Possible Questions to Ask in
First Team Leader Meeting

Outcome:

1. What outcomes or results do you specifically want to achieve by the end of the workshop? ...and overall, in the team building program?

2. What results or behaviors would you like to see or hear that you do not see now?

3. What is the cost or pain that's driving the need for those outcomes?

Obstacles:

1. Have you attempted to achieve these outcomes before? If yes, how? If no, what has changed to create the need now?

2. What or who has kept this outcome from being accomplished?

3. Why should these obstacles change?

Accountability:

1. What changes do you or your teammates need to make in order to ensure the team achieves these outcomes?

2. What support and commitment will you need from others?

3. What performance tracking system do you need to put in place to measure progress?

Report of Improvement Template

Our Goal or Outcome	

Information
   Start Date
   End Date
   Team Leader
   Teammates	

What Was Done	

Actual Improvement or
Results
   Measurable
   Non-Measurable	

Cost of Improvement
   Measurable
   Non-Measurable	

Suggestions for Future Projects or Outcomes	
Acknowledgment of Contributions	

RMT Implementation Plan – 4 Actual Examples

Example #1 Nuclear Power Generating Plant

Results: The senior leadership team created and deployed a 100-Day Behavioral Outage that transformed the employee culture. Using RMT's Work Agreement process and other tools, this courageous **improvement project** succeeded and was featured in *Nuclear News*.

Example #2 Field Support Team

Results: This self-managing team, in one year, increased its teammate trust by 78% and saved their organization $350,000 when they successfully used RMT's **behavioral Work Agreement** process and the Three Workshop Implementation Plan.

Example #3 International Project Team

Results: This major capital project team immediately saved $10,000 a week in labor costs when they successfully used RMT's **process Work Agreement** to streamline their meetings.

Example #4 Architectural Design Company

Results: This firm had a good problem. Their business revenue had increased 100% in the past twelve months. They grew from 50 to 100 employees practically overnight, and they were still growing. They needed a strategic plan and operating structure. Using **RMT's Three Workshop Implementation Plan** plus team **Work Agreements**, they succeeded.

Example #1

The first example describes our work with a nuclear power generating plant with 500 employees. They used many RMT processes – specifically team Work Agreements and the Right Choice "Accountability" Model.

This example is presented here a little differently than the other three. After you read a short synopsis, you will read an industry article from *Nuclear News* that described the seven behavioral modifications that compromised what that named their **100-Day Behavior Outage**.

Examples #2 - #4

I will show you how these teams used the Right-Minded Teamwork Three-Workshop Implementation Plan to achieve team improvement in the last three examples. Specifically, you will see what they accomplished in their **First** Workshop plus their **Second** and **Third** Workshops.

For each team, you will find a short description of what the team did as well as their actual Team Business Plan.

You don't need to conduct a detailed review of each plan.

Instead, use these plans as templates. These examples will give you positive ideas about creating your own Right-Minded Teamwork Implementation Plan and your Team Business Plan.

Example #1: Nuclear Power Generating Plant
Prairie Island's 100-day Behavior Outage

Synopsis

Facing a potential shutdown from their credentialing agency after a significant performance decline, Joel Sorensen, Vice President of the Prairie Island Nuclear Power Plant, knew things needed to change. So, he implemented Right-Minded Teamwork's Work Agreements and Right Choice "Accountability Model to support the plant-wide culture change plan.

Be sure to read Joel's comments in second modification about accountability and work agreements.

"If you had asked me 2 months ago if the leadership team would reach this level of performance, my answer would have been emphatically, "NO!" Now that we are on this road, I don't ever want to go back." ~ Joel Sorensen

Joel gave this interview to the *Nuclear News* that tells the story.

THE NUCLEAR NEWS INTERVIEW

Prairie Island's 100-day Behavior Outage

Changing employees' culture requires a site-wide plan and site-wide participation.

A 100-day outage at Prairie Island didn't shut down power production, but it did change the way the plant operates. Called a "Behavior Outage," the program was aimed at altering employee culture at Prairie Island. The outage ran from last August to November and was modeled after refueling and maintenance outages in having specific plans and goals.

The Behavior Outage has helped reduce human performance errors at Prairie Island. Outage plans called on employees to examine their attitudes while changing behaviors that contributed to unpredictable performance. *Joel Sorensen*, Prairie Island's site vice president, and his management team developed the concept for the Behavior Outage. They initiated it by first calling for an assessment of plant operations to highlight those areas where improvements were most needed. These included change management communications, accountability, leadership, human performance work practices, corrective action, work management, and outage preparation.

The two-unit Prairie Island plant, in Red Wing, Minn., is operated by Nuclear Management Company (NMC). The two units are Westinghouse pressurized water reactors, each rated at 535-MWe (net). The interview was conducted by Rick Michal, NN senior associate editor.

Could you explain the history of the Behavior Outage at Prairie Island?

I solicited some retired nuclear executives to help me understand where our organization was going, whether it was improving or not. Those executives came to Prairie Island the first week of August 2000 and did a self-assessment. As a result, a report they prepared showed that while plant performance had improved over the short term, our organizational effectiveness had been flat for a long time and was remaining flat. We used that report to spur our organization to break out of past behaviors and start moving ahead. The assessment showed that in order for us to have good long-term plant performance, we needed to have good behaviors on the part of our workers, managers, and supervisors.

How did you come up with 100 days for the outage?

We felt we needed to put some urgency on this. We didn't want another plan that would take months and months to execute and where we wouldn't see results. So, we decided to put together a plan to work on behaviors and get results within 100 days. Once we decided on a plan that had a sense of urgency, we decided to treat it like we would a plant refueling outage. For the Behavior Outage, there would be specific outage plans, outage schedules, and daily outage meetings to follow our progress. We patterned it after a refueling outage because we needed a similar way of doing business to get the results we wanted for our behaviors. We felt we could keep both units running safely while spending 100 days focusing on our behaviors.

What did it cost Prairie Island to conduct this outage, and did you bring in an outside vendor to help conduct it?

It doesn't cost much money to work on behaviors. We formed employee cross-disciplinary teams to help develop plans for each of seven focus areas we identified that needed improvement. These seven areas we called "behavior modifications." But we needed help because we were struggling with accountability as a behavior. So, we partnered with a private firm—**Lord & Hogan LLC, based in Houston, Texas [creator of Right-Minded Teamwork]**—to help us understand what accountability means and to work with us on accountable behaviors.

Could you talk specifically about your seven behavior modifications?

Most emphasis for behavior modification was put on our management team as leaders of the plant, but every part of the organization, from supervisors to workers, was engaged in this activity. I'll explain each modification individually:

Our first modification is change management communications, because we lacked a consistent way of implementing change. We put in place a change management model, which contains a step-by-step process, and we use it to implement all other changes we need to make. We also realized that communication had to be effective in order to instill these behavior changes across the organization, so we focused on improving internal communications between plant departments. The plan includes a mix of print, electronic, and face-to-face methods—with a strong emphasis on increased frequency of communications and greater supervisor communication with employees.

The second modification is accountability. During the 100 days, we worked on developing accountability agreements [now called **team Work Agreements**], which laid out how our managers should treat each other with regard to trust and respect. We also empowered a cross section of employees to go out and train their peers on the meaning of accountability. There is no financial incentive for living up to the accountability agreement, but what we find is that when we live these agreements, work becomes much more rewarding. We continue to adopt accountability agreements throughout the rest of the organization.

The **third modification** is leadership, and assessments were done for our entire leadership team. Every station manager received an assessment of his or her strengths and weaknesses. Each manager then developed a personal development plan, and they are now living and working that plan.

The **fourth modification** is human performance work practices. We put together two teams, one being a cross-section of workers and the other a cross-section of supervisors, that developed a common set of tools for use by plant employees to prevent human error events. These tools are self-checking, procedure use and adherence, communication standards, peer-checking, and "tail-gating" sessions.

Each **week during** the Behavior Outage we focused on one of these tools to help us understand how to use it in preventing human errors. For example, the "tail-gating" session is something we want all of our employees to work through before they start any task. We want them to be able to summarize the task, anticipate what might go wrong, foresee any consequences, and evaluate what tools could be used to prevent errors. It's a mental checklist for them to use and to discuss with their co-workers before they go out on any task.

Peer checking, of all of the tools, is the one I'm most impressed with regarding how the team came up with it. Peer-checking is common in the industry, but the twist our folks put on it is by actively caring. Generally, people in Minnesota are viewed as near the top in the nation in caring. To carry this active caring to the nuclear plant was innovative and something we continue to build on.

Our behaviors prior to the 100-day outage were "conflict avoidant," which meant that people would avoid conflict. But that has changed. I'll give you an example. A general laborer here recently confronted an operator who was standing above the top safety step on a ladder. This entry-level laborer said to the veteran operator, "Hey, you're not following the ladder safety practices. Why don't you let me help you down and I will help you find a ladder that is the right height for this job." Prior to this, it would have been easy for the laborer to walk by and not confront the operator on the ladder. But when that operator got down from the ladder, he turned to the laborer and said, "Thank you."

The **fifth modification** is corrective action, which plays off putting our accountability behaviors into practice. As an entire organization, we were allowing our corrective action backlog to become overdue, knowing it would grow. But strictly by using highly accountable behavior, we were able to complete 1410 corrective actions and 917 procedure changes in our backlog. We reduced our overdue items from about 300 corrective actions that were overdue to zero. These were all completed during the 100-day Behavior Outage. This was done strictly by holding people accountable, and by completing things when we said we would complete them.

The **sixth modification** is work management. Our human performance staff told us that if we didn't fix our work management process, we'd never be able to eliminate human performance events or equipment performance events. Our existing process had been burdensome and ineffective, so we put together a team to overhaul work management. That team learned we didn't have to start from scratch. There were already some good standard processes laid out here and we just needed to work on implementing them. The team put together an implementation plan within the 100 days by using our change management plan process. We are working now to implement the team's plan completely.

The **seventh modification** is outage preparation. In the past, we would allow outage milestones to come and go and not be met. But through accountability, we were, for example, able to make sure we met our pre-outage milestones in preparing for Unit 1's refueling outage last January. For that outage, we achieved approximately a 21 percent reduction in overall outage length compared to our refuelings over the previous 10 years encompassing 11 refueling outages. Much of that reduction was due to the preoutage preparation. I also credit it to the accountability behaviors on the part of our staff that executed the refueling outage—getting people to own issues, take actions, and commit to completion dates. I saw good results during the outage in the area of emergent issues that came up. Because of these accountable behaviors, we were able to identify, own, and correct emergent issues so they didn't become threats to the outage schedule.

How did the employees react when they were told there was going to be a Behavior Outage?

We had to create dissatisfaction with the status quo. I wanted everyone dissatisfied with the current state of affairs, the state of our organizational ineffectiveness. What we did was gather all the employees together for a "fire and brimstone" meeting to let them know we were not satisfied with the way things were working at Prairie Island. We all needed to change, including me.

We then laid out the plan and a new vision for the facility that focused on the long term. We had to get people thinking about what we needed to do to be an industry leader. We then set the plan in place, worked the plan, and at the end of the outage we celebrated the accomplishments.

As you went deeper into the Behavior Outage, did you see the culture changing among employees?

We, as an organization, started reading everything we could on changing culture. We recognized that our organization followed what the textbooks said about change: Roughly 20 percent of the organization jumps on board immediately and is helpful as change agents, about 50 percent of the organization sits on the fence waiting to see if it's "real" or not, and 30 percent resists change. We were aware we would need to face these resistors, but we didn't spend a lot of time on them. We focused instead on championing the change agents to help us drive the new culture.

With the Behavior Outage over, has the work force embraced the culture change?

What you're asking about is momentum. As a management team we recognize when we're letting the momentum slip, and I'm extremely pleased with our ability to recognize that. The management team owns that and jumps on it right away to make adjustments to keep the energy level up and the changes going. Can I say that we have driven to 100 percent on our change agents? No, but we continue to work hard at driving the highly accountable behaviors throughout all of our supervisors and entire work force.

Do you know if any other nuclear plants in the U.S. or internationally have conducted an outage like this?

Not to my knowledge. Certainly, organizations recognize that in order to get good results they need to have good behaviors. But it's difficult to drive those behavior changes throughout an organization.

Did any department at Prairie Island benefit more than others because of the Behavior Outage?

One of the things we're striving for is to break down "department silos" [isolation]. The fact that our managers think first as station managers and then as department managers puts a contrary spin on that question. I'd say the site benefited most by knocking the silos down between departments.

Is this type of outage going to be conducted at other NMC nuclear plants?

It's a matter of timing at each individual site. But the NMC is looking hard at modeling our accountability because we do want to work on accountability across our fleet of plants.

Has Prairie Island become a trendsetter by having a Behavior Outage?

When we return to being an industry leader, I will answer your question.

Example #2: Field Support Team

Synopsis

A Field Operations team for an international oil and gas production company operating in the Gulf of Mexico called and asked me to help them. They were responsible for supporting all the company's offshore oil platforms.

Though team members were competent, they weren't happy. And they were far from productive. Worst of all, two-thirds of the team members were arrogant and overly aggressive.

After identifying team business goals and psychological goals, I guided them toward creating two Work Agreements: a behavioral Agreement to improve trust and a process Agreement to become a self-managing team.

Just one year later, the team had completely turned around.

They had recommitted to their shared goals and were honoring their Work Agreements. As a result, they experienced:

- 78% increase in teammate trust
- 46% increase in mutual team member support
- 61% increase in complying with decisions
- Over $350,000 in savings

For a **more detailed description** of this team's first year with RMT, go to RightMindedTeamwrok.com, search for and read *How to Create Team Working Agreements That Bring People Together*.

First Workshop

I worked with this team for two years. We met every three months for a total of eight workshops. The first workshop was a two-day event; the others were one-day events.

In the first workshop, we created two Agreements.

The team's "relationships Agreement" addressed such things as proper communication, how to behave when a conflict occurs, and a commitment to resolve any unresolved teamwork issues.

The second Agreement addressed team meetings. Since the team had been recently instructed to become self-managing, conducting efficient and effective meetings was a top priority.

Second & Third Workshops

In the next two workshops, the team created a peer-to-peer assessment process. They also made team strategies that aligned with their profit center's strategic goals.

Below are their actual Team Business Plan and Work Agreements. The plan presented here was their second plan, created at the end of their first year.

Additionally, you'll see the results of their Team Performance Assessment Summary, which shows one full year of improvement data.

Large International Oil & Gas Company

Field Support Team's
- Safety & Tactical Plan
- Our Team Business Plan

Who We Are & What We Value

Our goal is to become a high-performing, self-managing team. This Team Business Plan includes the most updated perspectives and strategies for our team.

Who is the "Team?"
Mike: Facilities Representative
Will: Facilities Representative
Mark: Facilities Representative
Sam: Facilities Representative
Bob: Measurement Specialist
Steve: Workover Representative
Steve: Paint / Corrosion Representative

Our Commitment:

As a member of this team, I attest to being an active participant in creating this Team Business Plan and these Work Agreements.

I commit to hold myself accountable and to adhere to them to the best of my ability.

Field Support Team's Business Safety Plan

"Committed to Excellence in Safety"

1. **Full Implementation of STOP Program**
   A. STOP program to be used on ALL projects supervised. Encourage participation by contractor and operations personnel.
      a. Route all STOP cards through the MPS who will compile data and forward to E&S Champions for wide distribution of STOP recap report. Track contractor and company participation separately.
      b. MPS to use the graphical presentation of data for posting as per E&S format.
   B. Track "Near Misses" through the use of the STOP program.
      a. E&S Champions to track "Near Misses" on a separate recap report for use at weekly FSG meetings.

2. **Safety Meetings / Information-Sharing**
   A. Discuss safety issues during weekly FST morning meetings.
      o Standing agenda items.
         ▪ Review PDN policies or regulatory updates
         ▪ Review previous hitch safety-related issues
         ▪ Review Safety Alerts
      o Discuss working contractors' recent safety performance & practices to identify potential problems.
      o List action items.

B. Hold a pre-job meeting with contractor Supervisors and Safety Reps.

- Perform pre-job walk-through on-location with contract Superintendents, Safety Reps and Company Reps
- Perform hazards / safety risks assessment.
- Require ALL contractors to submit JSA before starting work in the field.
- Review the scope of work and safety guidelines.
- Hold a post-job meeting with key personnel and share Plus / Delta's with the group.

C. Daily "Operational" Offshore Safety Meeting

- Conduct meetings in cooperation with the contractor's Foreman / Supervisor / Safety Reps.
- Identify high potential hazards associated with day's planned activities.
  o Use JSA as a working document for daily safety meetings.
- Review previous day's Stop Cards.
- Include safety meeting topics and discussion in daily construction reports.
- Maintain a list of attendees. Keep a list in the job file.
- Perform Level 4 reviews as Standard Operating Procedure. Encourage operations participation.
- g. Conduct tailgate discussions throughout the day as the scope of work progresses to enhance safety awareness.
- Document on FST daily safety meeting forms.

D. Utilize E&S Champions.
- Work closely with E&S to review / critique / develop effective safety meeting agendas.
- Include E&S Champions in field trips to review job scope with contractors to help in identifying potential safety hazards.
- Include E&S Champions in ALL accident Root Cause Analysis.
- Include E&S Champions when possible, to assist in performing top side surveys to identify safety / compliance-related issues for maintenance work.

3. **Our Team Commitment**
   A. Full support of Team Interaction Agreements for Safety
   - Continue to participate in all team safety training & development workshops.
   - Increase focus on team success in safety.
   - Celebrate our accomplishments and acknowledge our opportunities to improve safety performance as a group.
   - Recognize our diverse workgroup. The team will support individual efforts in safety training and development for the good of the team.

   B. Provide effective communication of safety issues through Team Peer-to-Peer Process.
   - 100% team support of peer-to-peer efforts of honest, open, ongoing communication & feedback to accomplish our safety plan.

4. **Contractor Safety**
   A. Recognize outstanding contractor safety efforts and participation as appropriate.

Team Direction & Strategies

The four strategies listed below are the profit center's strategies. Included are our team's tactics and goals for addressing each strategy.

SS/EI Field Support Strategic Alignment Tactical Plan

Strategy 1 - Aggressively pursue implementation of PP&E

Champions & Responsibilities:
Will & Mark, they will:

- Collect and review all pertinent data every month to make sure the team is on track to accomplish yearly goals.
- Report back to the team.

Tactic 1: Continue to assess risk associated with construction projects through continued implementation of the FST Safety Plan.

Tactic 2: All members are trained in Root Cause Analysis. Perform RCA on near misses, ALL recordable accidents, and spills on construction and maintenance projects. Focus on information-sharing with peers and contractors.

Tactic 3: Continued support of the Contractor Safety Summary / Vendor Retention as a tool in contractor selection. Focus on feedback to E&S and Alliance sponsors on contractor performance.

Tactic 4: Continued use of Self-Review Process performing Level 4 surveys on all construction / maintenance / paint projects. Communicate efforts and results to operations and Facilities Engineers.

Tactic 5: Continue to require 100% reporting of accidents and environmental incidents.

Metrics:
1. Contractor Accident Incident Rate. Goal = IR 3.86
2. # Of Environmental Incidents due to construction. Goal = 2
3. # Of Level 4 Self Reviews performed. Goal = # of AFE projects supervised or greater
4. # Of RCA performed on incidents. Goal = 100% of recordables

Team Agreements
1. Each team member commits to accurate and timely reporting of contractor man-hours; all accidents, types, and number; environmental incidents; level 4 reviews; and all RCA's.

Strategy 2 - Proactively manage our portfolio.

Champions & Responsibilities:
Mike / Steve, they will:
- Track information and report back to the team.
- When the team is not meeting its metrics, the team commits to discuss and agree on how it can get back on track.

Tactic 1: Use surplus equipment and materials as available, utilizing procurement systems in place for determining availability.

Tactic 2: Work closely with FEs to develop AFE project objectives, cost estimates, and tracking processes to effectively meet goals. Examples: pre-job planning, daily cost reporting

Tactic 3: Active support and participation with FMTs in the MOC process.

Tactic 4: Work with Alliance Partners (suppliers) to achieve an inventory of needed stock for delivery in support of AFIS and vendor reduction efforts.

Metrics
1. Shut-in Time (actual vs estimated). Goal = +/- 15% (adjusted for changes in scope of work)
2. AFE costs (actual vs estimated). Goal = +/- 10% (adjusted for changes in scope of work)
3. $ saved by utilization of surplus equipment and materials. Goal = $100M

Team Agreements
1. Each team member will supply champions with needed data, i.e., enough information to justify adjustments for changes in the scope of work.
2. We gladly accept being held accountable for AFEs and downtime we help to plan.

Strategy 3 - Employ Total Quality Management (TQM) to manage our business.

Champions & Responsibilities:
Sam / Bob, they will:
- Announce dates for Alignment sessions and AFIS training.
- Track FST "paid-on-time" invoice statistics.
- Catalog FST Work Process Improvement documentation.

Tactic 1: Identify and prioritize key work processes by discipline, as necessary.
Tactic 2: Flowchart, measure, and improve key work processes that add the highest value to the team (80 / 20).
Tactic 3: Network with Field Support in WCPC to improve info-sharing of best practices and lessons learned.
Tactic 4: Active participation in updates of FST efforts and results at the Strategic Alignment Sessions.

Tactic 5: Support of Alliance Partners with a strong focus on feedback to sponsors in identifying opportunities for improvement.

Tactic 6: Continued consideration of small, disabled, and women-owned / minority businesses in the vendor selection process.

Tactic 7: Support of AFIS accounting system implementation and vendor reduction effort.

Metrics

1. Updates on efforts at Strategic Alignment Sessions. Goal = 3
2. Team participation in AFIS training and usage. Goal = 100%
3. % Of paid-on-time invoices. Goal = 88%
4. # Of key work processes measured and improved. Goal = 2 a year
5. # Of best practices workshops with WCPC field support reps. Goal = semi-annually

Team Agreements

1. Each person will give any work process improvements to champions.
2. Team members will provide evidence of support of the alliance partners and the use of small, disabled, or minority businesses through feedback documentation.

Strategy 4 - Build a committed team and become the "work location of choice."

Champions & Responsibilities:
Mark / Steve, they will:

- Track FST progress toward achieving our metrics and report back to the team.

Tactic 1: Continue informal PMP process as a coaching tool for individual and team performance. Conduct formal individual performance reviews / self-assessments, as necessary.

Tactic 2: Continue to develop and refine the "peer-to-peer" feedback process between team members.

Tactic 3: Continue to practice and refine customer / supplier feedback processes through effective post-job reviews. Focus on improved info-sharing of lessons learned.

Tactic 4: Participate in weekly crew change communication meetings and monthly FE meetings as needed.

Tactic 5: Continue formal team training sessions to improve team interaction and develop new skills.

Tactic 6: 100% commitment and participation by team members in FSG G&A cost-reduction effort. Full support of PC and BU initiatives and info-sharing with peers and O&M to understand and support business drivers guiding cost-reduction efforts.

Tactic 7: Develop consistent guidelines for contractor and company R&A / safety performance recognition to monitor and control costs.

Metrics

1. Team Interaction Questionnaire scores. Goal = 3 times a year
2. # Of post job reviews. Goal = 100% of construction / paint AFEs.
3. Formal Peer-to-Peer team communication exercises. Goal = semi-annually
4. 55% reduction in personal T&E.
5. Monitor cost associated with contractor & company R&A / safety performance recognition awards initiated by FST.
6. Review Team Business Plan semi-annually.

Team Agreements

1. Each team member commits to do their part in completing the above metrics.

Team Performance Factors

As a team, we agreed to evaluate ourselves every quarter and to use these performance factors to keep us on track.

Here are our subjective evaluation criteria:

√ +   = we are doing very well
√   = we are doing okay or average
√ -   = we need to improve; we're below average
-       = we are not doing this, or we are not doing this very well

Performance Factors   [one of their assessments]

1. We are a dynamic team constantly measuring our performance and contributions to the profit center. √
2. We function and interact at such a high level that adjusting our efforts as business needs dictate is an integral part of our process.√

3. As a team, we communicate and function as a "family" on all issues, knowing and trusting that we all have each other's interests in mind. √

4. We recognize and appreciate (value) our differences and similarities and honor our right to be individuals. √

5. We understand, as individuals with our personal preferences and feelings, that personal sacrifice for the good of the team will be a necessary part of our work at certain times. √

6. Our team interaction is at such a high level that sharing responsibility and accountability is never an issue. √−

7. Our personal and professional relationships among team members make recognition and celebration of each other's efforts a naturally occurring part of our team process. −

8. We are a leader in the safety and environmental arena because we adhere to our Field Support Team Safety Plan. √+

9. We have a team culture that is open, honest, and fun. √

10. We optimize available resources for our portfolio management by utilizing surplus equipment, sharing manpower, sharing expertise, etc. √+

11. We meet with customers regularly to discuss expectations, form partnerships, and gain feedback on performance. −

12. Each member knows and accepts their role and responsibilities as they pertain to the team. √

13. We take intelligent risks and explore new opportunities, ideas, and strategies. √

14. We understand our roles and are responsible and accountable for the performance of the profit center. √

Team Processes: Team Meeting Agreements

Agenda Field Support
Tuesday Morning Meeting

6:30 AM to 7:25 AM
Room 3193
Type of meeting
Facilitator:
Note Taker: Crew Change / Information Sharing

Agenda Topics
  A. Review Work Agreements for clarity and acknowledgments
  B. Technical Information Sharing
  C. Activity Recap
  D. PP&E - Performance Review
  E. Additional Agenda Items:

Team Processes: Peer-to-Peer Process & Agreements

Initially, the Facilities Reps developed the following principles for a Peer-to-Peer Process. Subsequently, the Field Support Team decided to adopt these principles for the entire team as an informal process (meaning no one was to be held accountable for doing these like on their PMP). The team intended to use these principles to improve overall team performance and team member interaction.

Guiding Principles:

1. **Defenselessness communication** - We want to be able to communicate about work situations without getting defensive ... so we can help each other solve / resolve problems. By so doing, we will improve our overall communication ability.
2. **Outside forces will not split us** - Whenever we have outside forces that have the potential to cause us problems (split us), we want to use the Peer-to-Peer Process to help us better understand each other's perspectives and learn how to prevent it next time.
3. **Tom** [their supervisor] **gets a consistent message from us** - We want Tom to get a consistent message from all of us. We also want him to see / believe we're achieving our potential. We intend to improve our working relationship with Tom.
4. **"Who better to talk to...?"** - We want to be able to talk to someone, like each other, who understands what we're up against.
5. **To learn timing and political correctness** - We want to use our discussions to determine on whom, and when, we can push back - like the business team, FMT's, etc. - without causing political and / or PMP problems for ourselves and our customers.
6. **Improve each other's working style** - We want to talk to each other and help each other improve our work styles versus trying to get others to change their style.

7. **Listen** - We want to really listen to each other... which doesn't mean we'll agree, but we won't let any disagreements get in the way of performing our jobs.

8. **Share information** - We intend to share the most appropriate information, realizing that schedules and work objectives get in the way sometimes. For example, it's important for people to attend our Tuesday meetings, but sometimes people can't come.

9. **We will not withhold** - If a teammate hears something about another teammate that's negative (or potentially negative), we'll bring it up to that person and / or the team as soon as appropriate. We intend to help that person and the team.

10. **The Peer-to-Peer is ours** - This process is to be used among ourselves, and it's not for PMP. However, we want it to help us improve in our PMP, avoiding any surprises that Tom might say to us - i.e., "so & so (OS) said ..."

11. **Talk to each other first** - If we have any problem amongst ourselves, we'll discuss it before others find out - especially Tom.

12. **It's an "inside job"** - We want to listen to understand versus listening to respond and judge each other. It's an inside job to notice we're getting defensive or judgmental. We're committed to "STOP" and really listen.

13. **Competitiveness is okay** - We encourage competitiveness, but it's not okay to try to make our light brighter by blowing out someone else's.

14. **We're proud to be a Field Support Team Member** - "I want to stop having to defend myself for being a member of the Field Support Team!"

Team Processes: Relationship Work Agreements

Agreement #1 Intention:

1. Each team member agrees to resolve or help resolve any / all team-related issues.

Conditions for acceptance / clarification:

A. It's our intention to be proactive with each other, to not let any issue go unresolved that would eventually cause problems, and to use this Agreement to improve team performance.

B. Whenever a team member has an issue to resolve, they will first go to others in private, and if they can't resolve it, then they will bring it up to the team.

C. Whenever two or more team members try to resolve an issue, each team member agrees 1) to listen to understand, 2) to swap roles and listen again 3) that no one will get defensive, 4) to express "what's needed," and 5) to resolve.

D. Resolving an issue means each team member will actively support team decisions and accurately represent those decisions to others.

E. We will not use words or body language that make the situation worse.

F. When we see a team member repeatedly breaking this Agreement, and it's a serious breach, we will: 1) address the problem in front of the group, 2) ask them what they feel is the problem, 3) as a group, explain what we feel is the problem, 4) try to resolve the problem, and 5) if we can't resolve, call in a mutually agreed-upon third party.

G. We'll watch our "zingers, joking, and cutting-up" with each other when there's a difficult or tense situation because it only makes things worse and hurts feelings.

H. If something is said and it hurts, "check it out" with them ASAP and resolve it.

I. If a team member needs to vent before they give another team member feedback or to resolve a conflict, it's okay to go to a third party, but it must remain confidential.

Agreement #2 Intention:

2. Each team member commits to support each other.

Conditions for acceptance/clarification:

A. We will review missed opportunities so we will not miss them again.
B. It's our intention to honor our commitment to each other so we can set the "standard" in CPDN.

Agreement #3 Intention:

3. Each team member will work to improve individual and team communications.

Conditions for acceptance/clarification:

A. We will communicate facts and clearly own when what we say could be opinions or assumptions.
B. We will listen to each other's opinions (and repeat it back) to make sure that we really hear each other. We intend to keep an open mind and to change our minds if appropriate.
C. If a team member checks it out with you, it's not about questioning that team member's commitment to the team. We just want to improve our one-on-one team communications.
D. We will not "badmouth" anyone, and we'll be open to feedback if others think we are.
E. When a team member experiences a problem, we'll own it, resolve it, and share the learnings with the team. We will not avoid or deny our role in it.

Team Processes: Team Performance Assessment Summary

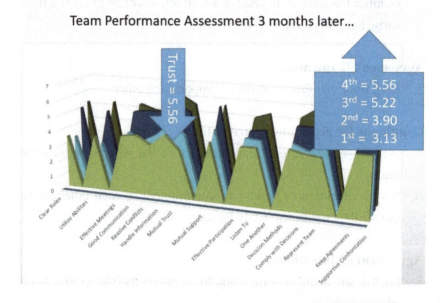

Team Performance Assessment 3 months later...

This Team's Results / Benefits ... After 1 Year

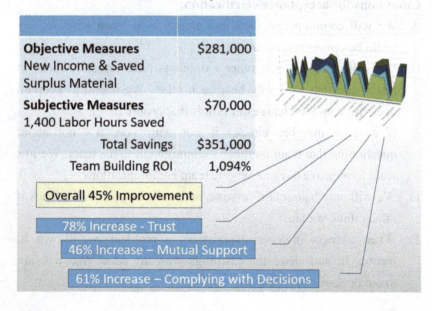

Objective Measures New Income & Saved Surplus Material	$281,000
Subjective Measures 1,400 Labor Hours Saved	$70,000
Total Savings	$351,000
Team Building ROI	1,094%

Overall 45% Improvement

78% Increase - Trust

46% Increase – Mutual Support

61% Increase – Complying with Decisions

Example #3: International Project Team

Synopsis

Without strong internal processes and teammate trust, teams fall apart.

Such was the experience of Peter and Randy, co-project managers of an 85-person major capital project team. This team was responsible for designing and building a billion-dollar chemical plant.

Twenty-five teammates were from the client organization, which owned the plant. The other teammates were from an international engineering company. All 85 teammates were in the same office.

Team members constantly disagreed over work processes, and toxic interpersonal relationships caused additional stress and dysfunction.

First Workshop

After conducting teammate interviews, I learned many teammates had complaints about the number of required team meetings. They felt meetings were ineffective and not valuable.

We decided this was the issue to address in the first workshop. With support, the team created Work Agreements that mapped out how they would use agendas, identified desired outcomes, and laid ground rules to keep meetings on track. They also addressed how to speak up if a meeting went sideways.

After just one month of living their new Work Agreements, teammates reported they were getting more work done because they were not in so many meetings, and the meetings they did have were more productive, organized, and better facilitated.

The team declared the Work Agreements a success, and managers Randy and Peter estimated **they were able to save $10,000 a week in labor costs.**

Second & Third Workshops

This team wanted to move quickly. They scheduled their second workshop just three weeks after the first. In that workshop, they wanted to address team communications.

And just two weeks after that, they conducted their third workshop, where they addressed prioritizing work.

Here is a summary of their team conclusions. Below, you'll find their Team Business Plan with Work Agreements.

Summary of Team Recommendations

1. Meeting Behaviors: commit to living the Agreement below
2. Type of meeting & frequency changes [see below]
3. PDN: follow agreed upon process [by June 11 training]
4. Weekly reports: change to bi-weekly
5. Make realistic promises between PMT / Client
6. Improve Client Communications: follow agreement below
7. Roles & Responsibilities: clarify as needed
8. QII: First Things First philosophy: commit to live
9. Teammates agree to follow issued plans and procedures.

Teamwork Issue: Meetings

Teammates: Darlene, Troy, Ernest

The Problem is...

a. There are too many valueless and unorganized (impromptu) meetings.

b. Our meetings are not efficient or effective.

c. There is lack of action item tracking and follow-through.

d. There is a lack of consistent meeting notes and no decision register or action item register.

The Opportunity is ...

a. To reduce total meeting time and use that extra time toward achieving our schedule.

b. To get more done in the meetings we attend – i.e., become more effective & efficient.

c. To increase our team's performance in completing action items on time.

The Actions recommended are ...

1. **Ask all teammates to follow the letter and spirit of our Meeting Process Agreement** (see Agreement in next section)

    a. Steps to endorsement:

        i. Present this Agreement and meeting frequency changes to PMT for feedback, modification, and agreement.

        ii. After PMT and Advisory team agree, leads will roll out the Agreement to all teammates and ask for their endorsement.

2. **Clarify types of meetings and frequency**.
   a. Summary of "Meeting" Recommendations:
      i. Reduce Morning Meeting to once per week; now called Weekly Meeting
      ii. Add Engineering Leads Meeting – conduct as needed
      iii. Capture Actions in IMS
      iv. BENEFIT: total time save is ~60+ man-hours per week

   b. **Weekly Meeting**
      i. Frequency & length: Monday, 10–11AM
      ii. Owner: Cary
      iii. Purpose: Ensure all staff are aligned for the week ahead
      iv. Agenda: Cary will publish if deemed necessary
      v. Scribe: Sara / PE will capture action items internal IMS, in real-time
      vi. Attendees: discipline lead, PMT, project engineers

   c. **Engineering "Issues" Meeting** - as-needed meeting
      i. Frequency & Length: this will NOT BE A PANIC MEETING. You will be given no less than 24-hours' notice.
      ii. Purpose: address pressing, and common issues as needed
      iii. Owner: Linda
      iv. Scribe: Troy / other will capture action items internal IMS, in real-time
      v. Attendees: if you are invited
      vi. Agenda: will accompany the notice

d. PMT - as-needed meeting

    i. Frequency & length: Every other Thursday 3:00 – 4:00 PM

    ii. Owner: Randy

    iii. Purpose: Discuss and clarify strategic issues such as task / role prioritization over the next 1-3 weeks

    iv. Agenda: Randy will publish if deemed necessary

    v. Scribe: Sara / PE will capture action items internal IMS, in real-time

    vi. Attendees: PMT

e. PDN / Value Improvement capture

    i. Frequency & Length: TBD - Tuesday 8:00 – 8:30AM

    ii. Owner: Linda

    iii. Scribe: Sara

    iv. Attendees: Project engineers, discipline leads, PMT

    v. Agenda: review last week's PDN

f. Value Added Improvement Meeting

    i. Frequency & length: TBD

    ii. Owner: Randy

    iii. Purpose: show clients how we add value

    iv. Agenda: TBD

    v. Scribe: Sara / PE will capture action items internal IMS, in real-time

    vi. Attendees: PMT

g. Procurement Meeting

    i.   Frequency & length: TBD

   ii.   Owner: Cary

  iii.   Purpose: Ensure orders are placed on time

  iv.   Agenda: TBD

   v.   Scribe: Sara / PE will capture action items internal IMS, in real time

  vi.   Attendees: PMT

h. Schedule Review Meetings

    i.   Frequency & length: TBD

   ii.   Owner: Randy

  iii.   Purpose: Ensure PMT is making progress

  iv.   Agenda: TBD

   v.   Scribe: Sara / PE will capture action items internal IMS, in real time

  vi.   Attendees: PMT

i. External Meetings

    i.   We recommend IOU teammates use the Meeting Process Agreement in all external meetings.

   ii.   We recommend that in the near future, when the PMT conducts an integrated team building workshop, the IOU presents this Agreement to the client and asks them if they would be willing to live by these practices.

Meeting Process Agreement

Team Choice:

1. Each teammate will do their part to ensure we have effective and efficient meetings.

Clarifications / Conditions for Acceptance:

A. All regularly scheduled meetings will have a clear purpose, clear outcomes, a realistic agenda distributed 24 hours in advance [identify preparation task], and the right people in attendance.

B. Regularly scheduled meetings will have a meeting owner who is responsible for facilitating and keeping the meeting on track. They will ensure proper meeting notes are taken and distributed.

C. Meeting closure: We will always restate our decision, understanding, and actions-owner-due-by-dates at the end of all meetings.

D. Action Items will be captured in IMS.

E. We agree to use the same level of efficiency and effectiveness in all informal meetings.

F. Everyone will make their thinking visible, even if it means expressing disagreement.

G. Meeting Ground Rules:
   - Show up on time, stay on task, and end on time.
   - "Let's take it outside." "Enough, let's move on."
   - Use the parking lot to capture important but not urgent ideas that will be addressed in future meetings or assigned to teammates to address.
   - Respectful and emotionally mature conversation.
   - None of us is as smart as all of us.
   - Come to a consensus even if you don't get everything you want.
   - Hold yourself and others accountable for living this Agreement.

Teamwork Issue: Communications

Teammates: Jackie, Tatiana, Johan, Michael

The Problem is...

a. There is disagreement as to what information needs to be documented and how.

b. The PDN process does not work effectively.

c. Some important information is withheld and / or not properly communicated from PMT to all teammates and vice versa.

d. There is no agreement as to when we need to use verbal or face-to-face communication as opposed to email or IMS.

e. There is a feeling of us versus them between engineering and PMT.

f. There is no agreed-upon way to express disagreement between teammates and leaders.

The Opportunity is...

a. To save time and to satisfy the client with a more effective PDN process.

b. To provide leaders and teammates with the right information at the right time.

c. To increase PMT and engineering collaboration.

d. To reduce misunderstandings and / or increase our likelihood of meeting the schedule because we are communicating properly, in emotionally mature ways.

The Actions recommended are…

1. **Create a behavioral Work Agreement** to address behavioral or interaction issues.

    a. The team will create the first draft (see below) and present it to the PMT for changes and eventual agreement.

    b. The teammates and the PMT leaders will cascade down this Agreement to all IOU teammates

2. **Improve client communication.**

    a. We recommend all teammates use the following "go bys" below to guide our client communications.

    b. We do this because there are times when verbal communications are sufficient and other times when communication needs to be documented.

    c. We recommend that our company provide more or additional training on how to use electronic project communications tools and software.

3. **Update weekly reports.**

    a. To add value and to save time, move to bi-weekly reports that are aligned with or sync with In-Control.

4. **Set realistic promises** between PMT and Client.
   a. Philosophy: Manage and adhere to the Quadrant II / First-Things-First model (see below).
   b. We recommend PMT first discuss deliverable due date promises with discipline leads before making promises to the client.
   c. If our discipline counterpart comes to you with last-minute requests, we will be firm. We can't accept last minute requests all the time. We don't want to accept bad planning on their part.
   d. We recommend all these because:
      i. It will help mitigate us vs. them (engineering vs. PMT).
      ii. It will help mitigate last-minute "drop stuff on my desk" incidents.
   e. We all agreed to the above.

5. **Clarify the IOU PDN process**.
   a. Leaders have discussed and agreed on the internal PDN process. The process will be vetted with the Client and then rolled out to all to follow.

Communications Agreement

Team Choice:
Each team member will communicate their thoughts and feelings in an emotionally mature and professional way.

Clarifications / Conditions for Acceptance:
A. We follow the spirit & intent of our One Way Values.
B. Emotional and professional mature communication can be described as tone of voice, word choice, body language, assertive versus aggressive, etc.
C. When we notice disagreement or tension in a conversation, we will stop and define terms or facts. We also commit to using the What to Say statements.
D. If we feel or believe another is being inappropriate, we will remind them of this Communications Agreement.
E. We also agree to give positive reinforcement to our teammates when we see or hear effective communication.
F. Not only do we agree to hold ourselves accountable, but we will also hold others accountable in a safe and supportive way, and that means we will speak up and not keep silent.
G. We don't condone behind-the-back negative conversation. We advocate that all teammates discuss their frustrations and resolve them.
H. If a team member continues to break any of our team Work Agreements, we will escalate this issue to a higher authority.

What to Say

Use these statements to advocate, inquire, or resolve conflict on any team.

Improved Advocacy

- Here's what I'm thinking and how I got there…
- Some of the assumptions I've made are…..

Improved Inquiry

- What data are you using to reach that conclusion…?
- What's leading you to make that conclusion…?

When You Disagree

- Tell me again how you came to believe this point of view.
- Are you using any data that I may not have considered?
- Am I understanding you correctly that you're saying…?

Dealing with an Impasse

- What do we know for a fact?
  - What do we think is true but don't have any data for yet?
  - Are there things we don't know?
  - What is unknowable?
- It seems / feels like we're at an impasse. Do you have ideas that might help us come to a new Work Agreement?

Teamwork Issue: Prioritize Work, Tasks, Packages

Teammates: Sumiti, Lora, Linda, Sharon

The Problem is...

a. There are too many last-minute requests that cause panic.
b. There are too many unrealistic requests / deadlines.
c. Too often teammates are not aware of and / or don't follow established procedures.

The Opportunity is...

a. To save time by reducing last-minute crisis situations and by being more flexible.
b. To increase our internal collaboration, plus our collaboration with our customers.
c. To create alignment between all IOU teammates and leaders as to what is realistic.

Statements of Fact...

a. When the Service Order is signed, and the schedule is published, prioritization will help.
b. Until the reorganization and alignments are published, there will be uncertainty in people's minds as to our priorities.
c. We believe that living the other sub-team Agreements will help resolve the "prioritization" issue.

The Actions recommended are...

1. **Adopt / agree to live by First-Things-First.**

   a. Ask all PMT leaders and leads to abide by the QII First-Things-First philosophy (see next section) and adopt it as an individual responsibility.

2. **Ask teammates to do the following.**

   a. If you believe you and your direct project supervisor are not aligned with respect to your work task prioritization, stop immediately to talk about it and resolve it.

   b. If you are asked by your direct project supervisor to stop what you are doing and do something else, seek to understand why. Maybe it is not really a crisis. However, if you go forward with the new task, be certain to negotiate and agree on what you will and will not do.

3. **Ask all teammates to follow the issued plans and procedures.**

   a. When gaps or misunderstandings are discovered, use accepted Client and Engineering Company procedures.

First Things First: A Time Management Philosophy

	Urgent	Not Urgent
Important	QI: Crisis, panic, pressing problems, missed deadlines, "fires" you have to address now	QII: Proper / realistic planning, crisis prevention, building positive relationships, having enough time to complete deliverables **Say YES!**
Not Important	QIII: Interruptions: hallway talk, last-minute requests for info Say No…	QIV: Low value or duplicate work Say No…
	Time	

Teamwork Issue: Roles & Responsibilities
Teammates: Sara, Carlos, Guillermo

The Problem is...

a. There is misalignment on roles and responsibilities in some areas.
b. There is confusion and lack of understanding of PMT roles and responsibilities.
c. Too often teammates don't feel empowered or engaged.
d. There is a feeling of us versus them between engineering and PMT.

The Opportunity is...

a. To improve effectiveness and efficiency by having a greater number of teammates and leaders aligned on roles and responsibilities.
b. To increase the likelihood of meeting the schedule because a greater number of teammates and leaders are following through on their roles and responsibilities.
c. To increase PMT and engineering collaboration.
d. To increase trust, accountability, and collaboration throughout the project team.

Statements of Fact...

a. We believe that living the other sub-team Agreements will help resolve the "prioritization" issue.

The Actions recommended are...

1. Realize we are currently in a re-alignment with our client.

    a. Some of the role ambiguity could be mitigated in the new alignment.

2. Empower individual teammates through growth.

    a. Growing individual capability is important. Therefore, we recommend PMT, and department leads do more to empower individual teammates to help them grow and develop.

3. Speak up if not in agreement.

    a. If any teammate or leader believes they are not in agreement with respect to their roles, responsibility, and duties, they have PMT's permission to speak to their direct supervisor.

    b. Follow these steps:

        i.   Review your roles as listed in the PEP.
        ii. Identify any changes you'd like to make such as where you believe you should have more empowerment.
        iii. Discuss with your direct project supervisor.
        iv. Come to an agreement.
        v.   If you can't come to an agreement, team leaders will make the decision.

4. Optional: Clarify roles through group activity.

    a. If deemed of value, use the following roles exercise.

    b. Consider a lunch-and-learn where all key roles are presented and clarified.

Roles & Responsibilities Team-Building Workshop Agenda

Desired Outcome: Discuss, clarify, confirm, and agree on who does what, when, and how.

Time Commitment: 2-4 hours
Participants: 7 teammates

Agenda
A. Kick-off
B. Agree on the Desired Outcome
C. Agree to believe and behave as one unified team
D. RMT's Role Clarification exercise
- One person at a time gives answers to the questions.
- Dialogue follows.
- Time permitting, create new Work Agreements & teammate understandings
- Capture conclusions in the Team Business Plan.
- If you run out of time, complete as many possible, then schedule a second session to continue.
E. Close

Example #4: Architectural Design Company

Synopsis

This is the story of an architectural design firm with over 100 employees. Leroy, the partner-in-charge, asked, "Can you facilitate one of those off-site meetings you do?"

I told him I'd be happy to. "What do you want to accomplish?" I asked.

He said he wanted to increase trust and to get the other founding partner to change his work behavior. The partner was driving everyone crazy. He was making customers angry. He was even running off some of their best employees.

My prospective client wanted his partner to stop all the whining and complaining. The company was having its best year ever, and he didn't want to blow it!

After I interviewed all the other partners and principles, I validated the head partner's perception. There was a lack of trust. The other leaders were also very frustrated with the other founding partner. Most believed that if he were gone, their problems would be solved.

I learned in the interviews that the organization had very little team and organizational structure. They had no strategic plan and no team operating system. Everyone agreed they needed a vision and more structure.

I reported back to the head partner and reflected what I was seeing.

I said, "Sometimes, the best way to address dysfunctional behavior is first to resolve work process issues. I recommend that in the offsite meeting, we create the organization's first strategic plan and operating structure. Once that is in place if a particular leader or partner doesn't do their part, then you can easily implement corrective action or termination."

He agreed to that plan.

First Workshop

In the first workshop, the team created five strategies, along with several process and behavioral Work Agreements. They even took the time to clarify roles and responsibilities.

They also agreed I would facilitate their leadership team meetings as part of the improvement process.

Second & Third Workshop

In place of additional formalized workshops, I facilitated the team's biweekly leadership team meetings for the next six months.

During our time together, we made our way through every one of Right-Minded Teamwork's 5 Elements. Below is their Team Business Plan.

Note: This final example has been abbreviated down to the essentials since there are already two preceding Team Business Plan examples, which include full details.

ABC Architectural Design Firm

Mission Statement

To provide quality architecture through personal service that responds to our clients' needs while providing a vibrant, positive environment for our employees.

Summary of Strategic Goals

Strategic Goal 1:
Deliver Exceptional Architectural Design & Service (details below)

Strategic Goal 2:
Be an Awesome Place to Work (details below)

Strategic Goal 3:
Increase Financial Value of Firm

Strategic Goal 4:
Expand Present Markets & Capture New Ones

Strategic Goal 5:
Contribute to Our Community

Strategic Goals

Strategic Goal 1: Deliver Exceptional Architectural Design & Service
Sponsor: Marc

Important Perspectives:
- Clients & prospective clients
- Suppliers / JVs / Contractors
- Community – a sense of pride in ABC's work
- ABC's employees – a sense of pride

Focus:
- Quality, innovation, TQM service to clients
- Creating a learning organization
- Vertical Studio work-process efficiency
- Efficient, competent, talented, and productive employees

ACTIONS

1.1: Create, implement, and follow an Exceptional Design Standard that will ensure we raise the bar on the level of our design.
  a. Describe & define the "exceptional" service standard.
  b. Train employees in 1) the ABC Exceptional Service Standard, and 2) capture specific service standards for each employee in their individual performance plans.
  c. Create and implement a client satisfaction "exceptional service" scorecard process to understand how ABC is doing and identify needed areas for improvement.

1.2   Maintain a continuous-improvement, total-quality process in all phases and levels at ABC.

Proposal & Contract Stage

a. Improve the entire proposal-to-contract process so both clients and ABC employees have a positive experience while creating clear deliverables, timelines, accountabilities, and other quality and service expectations.

Presentation Stage

a. Improve ABC's marketing presentation capability.

Job Stage

a. Fully implement the Vertical Team process.
b. Fully implement the QA / QC process.
c. Implement a web-based project management site for design and construction.

Follow-up Stage

a. Consistently follow-up on projects.

Strategic Goal 2: Be an Awesome Place to Work

Sponsor: Bob

Important Perspectives:

- Employees
- ABC management
- Clients / Suppliers / Industry

Focus:

- Just and fair rewards, benefits, and compensation
- Retention / turnover / recruitment
- Happy / satisfied employees
- The right people, with the right skills, in the right jobs, at the right time

ACTIONS

2.1: Ensure the right people with the right skills are in the right job at the right time and are delivering "exceptional architectural service."

    a. Create an awesome, effective, unified leadership team that is fun to work with.

    b. Establish and implement a partner peer review system using a Leadership 360 upward appraisal system.

    c. Agree on Associate's roles, and accountabilities.

2.2: Create an awesome, can-do, positive ABC culture and physical environment.

    a. Create and implement an annual, confidential employee perception survey (conduct two surveys in the first 12 months, then annually thereafter).

    b. Ensure the Employee Performance Review system is indeed helping the firm 1) have the right people with the right skills and 2) meet or exceed ABC's five Strategic Goals.

2.3: Develop and implement a standardized, flexible interviewing / hiring process using behavioral-based concepts, candidate accomplishments, and ABC's Strategic Goals.

    a. Develop minimum competency hiring standards for key positions.

2.4: Develop a leadership / employee training and development strategy that directly links to ABC's five Strategic Goals.

    a. Leadership: Using the leader upward appraisal / individual improvement plan, the firm will support / fund the leader to attend training to improve leadership skills.

    b. Employee: Using the individual performance reviews and the (potential) employee survey to identify needed training, the firm will support / fund training and development courses for employees.

    c. Improve communication of office procedures, standards, and policies.

2.5: Ensure ABC has a just and fair rewards and compensation system.

    a. Assess the current formal and informal compensation system that will help ABC meet or exceed its Strategic Goals.

2.6: Celebrate our company, team, and individual successes.

    a. Create ways to celebrate with our clients, suppliers, and employees.

Sample Roles & Responsibilities

Example 1: Leroy

What do I contribute to the firm?
- Leadership through final decision-making when required to resolve issues
- Personal and professional presence in the community through volunteer organizations and political activities
- Primary networking, public relations, and project procurement effort
- Provide the glue to hold the organization stable

What authority do I currently have?
- President and chairman of the board of directors
- Own majority of voting stock
- Can make final decisions (only with the majority of board vote)

What do I need?
- Need no further authority and feel no boundaries within the framework of what we all agree to as the best interest of the firm

Leroy: What Will I...

START

1. Be more organized: delegate direct project-related issues, solicit feedback regularly from principals, receive feedback from principals regarding when I am being impulsive
2. Push/direct people back to solving own interpersonal relationships
3. Spend more time with employees, getting to know them – dedicating the time to personally interact and recognize contributors
4. Trust all principals in their judgment and level of interest – demonstrate support when delegating, self-monitor behaviors when delegating, forgive the failures, negotiate timelines and expectations, receive, and listen and positively respond to push back from Principles
5. Share more of the public image of the firm – communicate when events "expect" attendance and when they "may" attend – ask for what is needed, and discuss with Mark to determine in Monday management meeting; ask people to go to events "with me"
6. Be more patient with employees and Principals – ask for feedback and coaching; increase self-awareness of body language and tone of voice
7. Recognize that everyone doesn't think and make decisions like me – raise self-awareness, self-monitor reactions to different styles, rely on trust

STOP

1. 1Being stressed out by daily situations – focus on the "start," delegate project-specific issues, personally commit to making the mental shift; double-check when delegating actions
2. Being impatient – (see above)
3. Working 12-hour days – schedule a vacation; make the mental shift that it won't end if I give responsibility away
4. Letting the activities and demands of our clients control my life – reprioritize events and communicate priorities to peers

CONTINUE

1. To provide leadership and vision for the firm
2. Mentor those I feel have the ability and drive to succeed
3. Make the firm financially successful by obtaining high-profit projects
4. Take the image of the firm to the highest level possible
5. Follow my plan to dispose of my stock in the firm and retire

Example 2: Bob

What do I contribute to the firm?
- A liaison in computer technology between users and non-users of CAD (because I took it upon myself to understand the system and its implications)
- Heavily involved in staffing human resource functions
- Agent of change for policies that beg to be implemented because they have been successfully used by other companies whose growth rates have similarly demanded change
- The implementer of solutions that are necessary to achieve the goals and vision of the company
- Represent this firm as one of its leaders

What authority do I currently have?
- Review and make recommendations for software and equipment purchases related to CAD
- Suggest alternatives in our policies and decisions
- PIC lead committee member for human resources
- Draft proposals for projects and give input to others when asked

What do I need?
- Receive input and increase staff before a crisis occurs
- Change the culture in ways beneficial to the firm
- Support of all other Principles in enhancing our image through understanding and dedication to quality programs and policies

ABC Architectural Design Process Work Agreements

1. Each Principle will either print their own budget reports OR provide a list of job numbers to their accounting contact person to get the budget reports.
   - Schedule time with the Project Manager to discuss budget and completion reports.
   - Create a plan of action; ensure that the Project Manager understands where they are on the project and what needs to happen to ensure a quality project is delivered within budget and on time.
   - PIC meets with PMs twice per month.

2. "Design people" (Leroy, Mark, Marc, Cheryl) will meet together to decide what to do with controversial designs during the proposal phase.
   - What can we do within the budget?
   - How much are we willing to invest of ABC's money?
   - Do we go back to the client & sell the design to get more money?
   - If it is determined that the project will require an ABC investment, present to Management Team for: Approval Veto, Alternative solutions

The team also made two additional process Agreements two weeks later:

3. Print and establish a list of PIC, PM to input into the Win2 system.
    a. Ensure Ralph checks the list for accuracy.

4. We agree that if we cannot accomplish the outcomes & accountabilities, we agreed to, we will raise the issue with Principles to re-evaluate & prioritize

And, after another four weeks, the team added another three process Agreements:

5. Discuss Aged Receivables at the last Management Meeting each month.
    a. Accounting to provide Aged Receivables to Stephanie by Wednesday prior to distribution and review.
    b. Each Principle agrees to review the Aged Receivables Report prior to the Management Meeting.
6. A report will not be labeled "final" until an assessment of the accounting system has been made and agreement by Management Team has been reached regarding how the "profitability" of a project is reported.

7. Every two weeks in our Management Meeting, we will discuss Forecast Staffing Needs (at the end of the meeting).
    a. We agree that Ralph should be present for this portion of the meeting.
    b. Leroy should share any relevant information early on and is excused from this portion of the meeting.

Architectural Design Action Work Agreements

Intention:

1. When we discuss and agree on our individual roles and responsibilities, we will be open and honest (in a business context); we will address the issue and not attack the person.

Conditions for Acceptance / Clarifications:

- None were made for this Agreement.

Intention:

2. Each team member agrees to address issues without getting defensive.

Conditions for Acceptance / Clarifications:

A. If someone does get defensive, it's okay if we acknowledge it, quickly apologize for it, and move on.
B. It's not about being perfect. It's about recovery and rebounding.
C. If someone does get defensive, we will:
    - Reframe the issue
    - Ask, "Are you feeling defensive...?"
    - Say, "I'm sorry, but I don't think you understand my point...will you reflect back to me what you're hearing me say?"

Intention:

3. We will discuss and agree to upfront on the ABC direction we are going, and we will all visibly support that decision.

Conditions for Acceptance / Clarifications:

A. If we feel a Principal has not upheld this Agreement, we will bring it up with that Principal and remind them of this Agreement. We will provide behavior-specific and / or specific examples of instances when we perceived this Agreement was not being upheld. We will resolve the issue.

B. Our intention for this Agreement is to be unified outside this room, and when we have disunity, we work it out in this room.

Intention:

4. We will address each other one-on-one when there is a difficult issue with the intent to resolve and reach an agreement.

Conditions for Acceptance / Clarifications:

A. If we cannot reach an agreement, we will raise difficult issues in a group setting with the intent to reach an agreement. We will not engage inside conversations with the intent of avoiding or politicking.

Intention:

5. If a Principal feels that they are overloaded and cannot perform all the tasks or meet all the expectations, they will call it out at the Management Meeting.

Conditions for Acceptance / Clarifications:

   A. If we perceive a Principal is overloaded and is not meeting expectations, we will call it out.
   B. Our intention for this Agreement is to create the right work workload balance to meet our Strategic Plan.
   C. Whenever possible, we will educate / inform each other on our current workload (increase understanding of what is on each other's plate) so that we improve our work efficiencies, like reducing callbacks.

Intention:

6. We will not engage in negative discussions about another Principal.

Conditions for Acceptance / Clarifications:

   A. If a Principal speaks negatively about another, we will stop them and encourage them to work that issue out with that Principal.
   B. We will provide assistance and guidance in helping each other go back to the source and reach an agreement.

Roles & Responsibilities

Facilitator

- Plan meeting and build and distribute the agenda before the meeting.
- Develop and present for agreement the purpose and desired outcome(s) for the meeting.
- Learn and incorporate team members' key desires for participation in the overall meeting purpose and outcomes.
- Build consensus for desired outcomes before the meeting.
- Ensure the right people are invited to the meeting.
- Design the room layout to support meeting outcomes.
- Set a positive tone with clarity, communication, and demeanor.
- Ensure everyone gets heard.
- Observe group dynamics and guide the group towards achieving meeting outcomes.
- Assist people in resolving misunderstandings or conflicts.
- Be actively involved in discussions without asserting opinions or personal positions.
- Ensure the desired outcomes are achieved.

Team Leader or Sponsor

- Accountable for the overall productivity of the team/project.
- Request that a facilitator (either from within the team or outside the team) facilitate team-building efforts.
- VERY important: Discuss and agree with the facilitator how the facilitator should call out inappropriate team leader behavior, if required, during the meeting.
- Clearly understand the facilitation deliverables and timeline for completion.

Participants

- All participants are equally responsible for the success of the meeting, including achieving desired outcomes.
- Read the agenda before the meeting and come prepared with any brainstorming lists or presentations.
- Contact the facilitator if they feel like they don't need to participate in this meeting and work out a mutually agreeable solution.
- Stay engaged in the meeting's discussions and ask others to stay engaged if they begin to "check out."

Scribe

- While facilitating Work Agreements, the facilitator plays Scribe, Timekeeper, & Tangent Monitor roles
- Capture all the relevant meeting information and display it publicly. Relevant information may include Work Agreements, prioritizations, project reports, action items, etc.
- Bringing clarity to confusion, often by hardly saying a word.
- Think about how to best organize meeting information, make it visible for all to see, and help people put words to their ideas while staying true to their voice and content.
- Honor the original intent in all notes captured.

Timekeeper

- Assist the facilitator in monitoring the time.

Tangent Monitor

- Help the group monitor when the discussion goes off in a different direction and help bring the group back to the subject.

Work Agreements
A Narrative of the 10 Facilitation Steps

In this section, you will find a narrative description of the ten steps. To learn how to facilitate Work Agreements, go to RightMindedTeamwork.com or your favorite book retailer and pick up *How to Facilitate Team Work Agreements*: *A Practical, 10-Step Process for Building a Right-Minded Team That Works as One.*

· · · · ·

Let's start by assuming a team leader has decided to conduct a one-day Work Agreements workshop and has asked you to facilitate. Here are your preparation and facilitation steps.

First Decide: In-Person or Virtual Workshop?

If you must conduct a virtual workshop, the same principles, concepts, and steps presented here still apply. Use a video software conferencing platform to ensure all participants can see each other and the virtual flip chart used for capturing your team Work Agreements.

However, **an in-person workshop is the superior choice** because teammates can see and feel each other's attitudes and behaviors.

Preparation Steps 1-3

Take these steps before the workshop.

1. Agree on the first teamwork topic to address, which will result in a Work Agreement.
2. Determine the topic's desired outcome.
3. Design an opening question to be asked to kick off the topic dialogue.

In **Step 1,** the team leader informs the facilitator what they want to achieve and why.

Often, some difficult situation has occurred that has precipitated the desire for this workshop. After you understand the leader's desired teamwork outcomes, you interview all teammates to understand what they want to achieve and why.

After the teammate interviews, you share the team's collective input with the leader, which results in selecting teamwork topics to address in the first workshop.

In this book, we use two outcomes as teaching examples: improving communication and team decision-making. The first is a behavioral issue, and the second is a work process issue.

In **Step 2,** an agenda is created that includes the desired outcomes.

In **Step 3,** an opening question is created for both issues: communication and decision-making. In the workshop, the facilitator asks those questions to launch a team discussion. Eventually, this discussion leads to one or more Work Agreements.

Facilitation Steps 4-10

4. When the time is right, ask the opening question for your topic.
5. Capture legitimate behavioral answers on a flipchart.
6. Write and propose an intention statement.
7. After a short dialogue, ask if teammates agree to live the intention.
8. Write clarifications and conditions for acceptance.
9. Create an interlocking accountability condition.
10. When everyone approves the Work Agreement, celebrate. Move to the next topic.

The Workshop

Imagine you are 10 minutes into your workshop. The team leader has welcomed everyone. All teammates have agreed to the desired outcomes, agenda, ground rules, Decision-Making Agreement and the day's logistics.

Before you ask your opening question, take five minutes to introduce the Right Choice Model. Your goal is to present the model in such a way that when you finish teaching it, all teammates declare,

> *Of course, we need to approach [our issue] in a Right-Minded, accountable way. Let's get started.*

Another option is the team leader could present the Right Choice Model by relating it to a current difficult team challenge.

Either way, after you present it and the team's collective "Decision-Maker" has made that commitment, it is the right time for you to ask the opening question.

To learn more about the Right Choice Model and how to apply it in your team, go to RightMindedTeamwork.com or your favorite book retailer, and pick up **How to Apply the Right Choice Model**: *Create a Right-Minded Team That Works as One*. Within the book, look for the section titled, "How to Present & Apply the Right Choice Model in Your Team." There, you will be given specific instructions on how to present the Right Choice Model successfully, including how to relate it to your team's current challenge.

Asking the opening question officially starts an honest discussion on the first teamwork topic - **Step 4**. Here is a good opening question: *If we communicated respectfully, what would you see or hear teammates say or do, or not say or do?*

Up to this point, you have been doing most of the talking. After asking the opening question, you move into listening, observing, and facilitating.

Now that the opening question has been asked, you listen to the team's discussion, which may last 30-60 minutes. All the while, you are capturing legitimate behavioral answers on a flipchart - **Step 5**.

In **Step 6**, while teammates continue to discuss their workshop topic, you think about and write an intention statement. The proposed statement should evolve from the team's list of answers. When the time is right, you suggest the intention statement. Here is an example: *Each teammate will communicate in a respectful way with each other and our customers.*

In **Step 7**, you ask teammates if they will agree to live the proposed intention. Most of the time, teammates agree. But they usually believe it needs more work. It is still a work in progress.

In **Step 8,** the team discusses their specific clarifications or conditions for acceptance of the intention statement. As teammates add and edit their conditions, you and the team leader periodically ask them, if they truly lived their Work-Agreement-in-progress, would they achieve their desired outcome? Most of the time, they will say yes. This "yes" motivates the team to continue making the "right" Agreement for this team.

Finally, **Step 9** calls for "interlocking accountability" within the Work Agreement - a vital step to encouraging the team to live their agreements day in and day out. Fortunately, you will only need to create interlocking accountability once. It will apply to all Work Agreements.

For a real-world example of interlocking accountability, flip back a few pages to the section "Real Team Work Agreements" and look at the final condition in the behavioral Communication Agreement.

In **Step 10**, every teammate publicly commits to hold themselves and others accountable to upholding the team Work Agreement. At this point, everyone should all genuinely believe the Agreement will help the team achieve its goals.

It's important to note that it's not unusual for people to break their Work Agreements after the workshop. Often, this breach is just an honest mistake, or a habit not yet transformed. However, if a teammate continues to break a Work Agreement, the team should have an agreed-upon condition [step 9's interlocking accountability] that clarifies how they will confront one another.

Real Team Work Agreements

Below you will find two real examples. The first one is a **behavioral** team Communication Work Agreement. The other is a **process**, Decision-Making Work Agreement.

I worked with this team for a few years. They were phenomenally successful Agreements because teammates passionately created and actively lived them day in and day out.

The communication Work Agreement directly below is also used as a teaching device in the book *How to Facilitate Team Work Agreements: A Practical, 10-Step Process for Building a Right-Minded Team That Works as One.* In that book, I will show you, with a few editorial privileges, how that team created this Agreement.

Behavioral Agreement – Communication

Team Choice: Intention Statement
   1. Each teammate will communicate in a respectful way.

Clarifications / Conditions for Acceptance:

  A. We will use good communication techniques that include appropriate body language and tone of voice, plus suitable words.
  B. If we see or hear disrespect or we hear an inappropriate behind-the-back conversation, we own it and need to step in.
  C. If someone unintentionally shows disrespect, we will give them the benefit of the doubt, let them know, and create a new way to interact going forward.
  D. We will actively support team decisions in word, deed, and energy; we will use our decision-making protocol agreement for key decisions.
  E. We will be on time for meetings.
  F. We will ask, "May I interrupt you?"
  G. We will use observable facts during disagreements and decision-making, and we will acknowledge when we are using assumptions.
  H. We will understand each other's roles, ask for help if we need it, share relevant information and if helpful, give constructive feedback in private.
  I. If someone continues to break this agreement, we will tell them that we will invite a third party to help if there is continued disagreement. If that doesn't solve the issues, we will all go to a higher authority for support and resolution.

Process Agreement – Decision-Making Protocol

Team Choice: Intention Statement

2. We will go for consensus for all key team decisions, but our fallback will be that Maria [team leader] will decide if we cannot reach a consensus.

Conditions for Acceptance / Clarification

A. Before entering a discussion, we'll agree on the decision-making method and fall back, plus when [date] a decision will be made.

B. Before delving into a solution, we will create an opportunity or problem statement.

C. At the beginning of our discussion, we will determine boundaries & givens (i.e., time sensitivity; cost, hassle, impact, 80% or 100% perfect decision, etc.).

D. We provide a business case (appropriate justification) for our decision, including cost/benefit.

E. During our conversations, we will advocate and inquire. We will not hold back. For instance, we will acknowledge assumptions and facts.

F. To create the best solutions, we will also think about alternative ways to test our solution (Devil's Advocate).

G. If we find ourselves at an impasse, we will call a "time out" to calm down or acquire more technical information.

H. When a decision is made, we will accurately represent and support the decision.

I. We do this agreement because we want to improve teamwork and trust in one another.

J. We will hold ourselves and others accountable for living the letter and the spirit of this agreement; we will fine-tune it as necessary

Work Agreements
That Bring People Together as One

This summarizes how a team used the Team Perception Survey as one of their methods to track actual performance. It's also a testament to the transformative power of team Work Agreements.

To read a more detailed account of this team's success, go to RightMindedTeamwork.com/blog and search for *How to Create Team Working Agreements That Bring People Together.*

. . . . .

Tom was the Manager of Field Operations for Chevron in the Gulf of Mexico, responsible for supporting all the company's offshore oil platforms. He was good at his job. But one of his teams was struggling.

Though they were competent, they weren't happy, and they were far from productive. Worst of all, two-thirds of the team members were arrogant and overly aggressive.

Tom didn't know what to do, but he'd gotten help from Dan Hogan, Chevron's long-standing external team building facilitator in the past. So, he called Dan again.

After identifying business goals and psychological goals, Dan guided the team to create two Work Agreements: a behavioral agreement to improve trust and a process agreement to become a self-managing team.

Just one year later, the team had completely turned around. They had recommitted to their shared goals and were honoring their Work Agreements.

As a result, they experienced:

- 78% increase in teammate trust
- 46% increase in mutual team member support
- 61% increase in complying with decisions
- Over $350,000 in savings

Most importantly, they were happy and productive, which also meant their leaders and the team's customers were happy.

The team continued to improve and work together for another five years, never returning to their old, dysfunctional ways.

This Team's Results / Benefits ... After 1 Year

Objective Measures New Income & Saved Surplus Material	$281,000
Subjective Measures 1,400 Labor Hours Saved	$70,000
Total Savings	$351,000
Team Building ROI	1,094%

Overall 45% Improvement

78% Increase - Trust

46% Increase – Mutual Support

61% Increase – Complying with Decisions

The End

On behalf of **Reason** and all the **Right-Minded Teammate Decision-Makers and Team Facilitators**, we extend our best wishes to you and your teammates as you create another *Right-Minded Team that Works Together as One*.

CPSIA information can be obtained
at www.ICGtesting.com
Printed in the USA
LVHW082353290122
709758LV00011B/489

9 781939 585127